THE

PHILOSOPHY OF MORALS.

THE

PHILOSOPHY OF MORALS;

AN INVESTIGATION,

BY A NEW AND EXTENDED ANALYSIS,

OF THE FACULTIES AND THE STANDARDS

EMPLOYED IN THE

DETERMINATION OF RIGHT AND WRONG:

ILLUSTRATIVE OF THE PRINCIPLES OF

Theology, Jurisprudence, and General Politics.

<hr>

BY ALEXANDER SMITH, M.A.

<hr>

IN TWO VOLUMES.

VOL. I.

LONDON:

SMITH, ELDER AND CO., 65, CORNHILL,

BOOKSELLERS TO THEIR MAJESTIES.

1835.

PREFACE.

Wherein consist *Right* and *Wrong?* — By what test or criterion may we, in doubtful or disputed cases, determine what is any one's duty or right? — are questions, which, even were the solution of them not often required for practical purposes, must always form a subject of deep philosophical interest.

Moral, or ethical science is, in a confined, but, I believe, more common sense, understood to have regard principally to the private duty of individuals; and, in this way, it is associated, in the minds of many people, with disquisitions on temperance, chastity, truth, honesty, diligence, and the like. But to have an idea of the full interest

and importance of the science — (not meaning
that the topics now alluded to are uninteresting
or unimportant, otherwise than from their triteness
and familiarity) — it is necessary to take a wider
view of it — as embracing every question of *right*
and *wrong* — every question of what is just — fit
— reasonable — fair — proper — that can arise out
of any possible relation between one being, or
collective number of beings, and another being, or
number of beings — from the Deity down to the
meanest insect: — every question relating to the
just and fair *rights*, or *powers*, or *privileges*, which
one being can claim over, or from another. In
this way the science of ethics forms a basement,
at once, to those of theology, jurisprudence, civil
and criminal, and politics, — or all that regards
the moral justice of laws and government — human and divine. — Never, perhaps, was there a
time, when there was more frequent discussion of
points relating to these momentous topics, or
more need of all the enlightenment that philosophy can shed upon them; and I cannot help
expressing my wonder, by the way, that while
men (whether beneficially or not) seem intent on
divesting themselves of all the trammels of pre-

scription in political affairs — making truth and reason every thing, authority and custom nothing, — there seems an equal disposition, in religious matters, to make a sacrifice of the plainest dictates of common sense, and the clearest truths of revelation, to the most anile prejudices and superstitions.

The question as to the *ultimate criterion* of right and wrong, has always been more or less mixed up with the other, and more metaphysical, inquiry, which relates to the nature of the *mental operation* by which moral distinctions are perceived. Indeed the two questions have, even by some of the most acute inquirers, been treated as one. How this confusion (for such I think it) has arisen, will appear in the course of this work. At present, it is sufficient to notice the fact ; and to observe that, even had the two questions been always kept apart, a theory of moral distinctions which did not embrace the consideration of both, could not be viewed but as materially defective. — These two questions together may be taken to comprehend all that relates to what is called the *Philosophy of Morals*.

It is now a good many years, since, partly from

a desultory curiosity, partly from the relation of the subject to my professional pursuits, my attention was attracted to this branch of science. A very cursory examination of existing systems sufficed to create an impression on my mind, that the subject was capable of receiving much additional light. It appeared to me, that, in all the discus-.sions I had seen, wherever what appeared to me the *truth* was stated, it was stated but indefinitely, and even inaccurately ; — that it was scattered over a variety of contending arguments ; — and that, to reconcile these, and distinguish, in each, the sound from the unsound, there was room and occasion for a more minute and exact analysis, than had yet been attempted, of the moral perceptions — both in regard to their nature, as mental acts, and their subjects as a species of truth. It seemed to me in short that, if the chief problems in the theory of morals had been solved at all, the true solutions were yet insufficiently distinguished from such as were erroneous : those insufficiently vindicated, these insufficiently exposed : — that, even if upon bases not entirely new, there was scope for a new classification of phenomena ; that new junctures and connexions were required — new harmonies and fittings ; — in short, a new combination — a new system. It need not then be reckoned a derogation from the value of such a work as this, that it does not offer what might be called a *new theory* — as meaning that the more considerable of the doctrines maintained are such as havè never been stated before. A new theory, in this sense, might, indeed, at this time of day, be safely set down as a false theory. There are few of the more considerable problems in theoretical morality, of which the true solution may not *somewhere* be found. But truth not established, is truth not known ; and he who can distinguish, among a variety of statements pretending to be true, and each having its share of acceptation as true, which is really true — may not unfairly claim to rank as a discoverer. — Whether I have done this or not, is another question. I now vindicate the purpose — not the execution.

It has always been a favourite mental exercise with me, to examine and compare various processes of reasoning employed on the same subject : — to discern, amid apparent contradiction, when they moved (so to speak) in parallel lines — each

establishing really independent and consistent
conclusions ; — when (to continue the metaphor,)
starting from different points, they ultimately con-
verged to the same result ; — when, starting together, they diverged into various, but not con-
flicting issues ; — and, finally and chiefly — in the
case of their crossing or becoming implicated with
one another — where, in any of them, was the
exact point of divergence from the truth, by the
correction of which the subsequent knots and perplexities might be disentangled. To a taste for employment of this kind, such a subject as ethical philosophy promised full scope. Always finding, however, a greater pleasure, as respects such subjects
as *thought* alone is the instrument of investigating,
in speculation, than in reading — the mode in
which I felt disposed to enter on the pursuit I had
chosen, was that recommended by Paley : — not,
however, on account of his recommendation (for
it was then unknown to me) but because it promised most entertainment to myself. It is thus
he describes it : —

" My method of writing has constantly been
this : to extract what I could from my own stores
and my own reflections in the first place ; to put

down that, and afterwards to consult, upon each subject, such readings as fell in my way : which order, I am convinced, is the only one whereby any person can keep his thoughts from sliding into other men's trains."

Accordingly, after having obtained, by a cursory perusal of some of the principal theories of morals, a general notion of the problems to be discovered, and of the more material points of dispute to which they had given rise, I thenceforth left, for a time, my instructors, and proceeded to explore the almost unknown region by myself; nor did I again return to them, for the purpose of asking directions or otherwise, until I had enabled myself to compare observations with them on an equal footing, and as one who had personally travelled over the same, or as great an extent of territory as themselves. If, by this method, I have sometimes lost my way, and wandered far about, in order to arrive at a point to which a guide would have conducted me by a short route, I have, in return, seen many sights I should otherwise have missed; gained a better knowledge of the country in general, and the relative position of its various localities; and, sometimes, it may be, fallen upon a shorter cut than the ordinary track would have furnished.

Some of my statements, then, though corresponding, perhaps to the letter, with those of other writers, have really been, in respect to the mode of their formation, original; and I have reason to suspect that I have, in a few instances, uttered, with the air of one who produces a novelty, sentiments which are neither new nor unknown. In disavowing any intentional attempt to claim credit for discoveries already appropriated, and in explaining what may have occasioned the appearance of such intention, I trust I shall be reckoned as offering a sufficient apology for what, perhaps, after all, is but an insignificant trespass. Even where I may be found in the closest company with another, I think it will be seen that I have joined him by a road of my own.

I may now just briefly allude to the chief subjects discussed.—For some years past, the current of philosophical opinion has seemed to me to run somewhat decidedly in favour of the hypothesis that moral approbation, or its contrary, must resolve ultimately into a *feeling;* and that any thing of a thinking or reasoning character which takes place, is of a subordinate and preparatory kind — fulfilling, as it were, merely the office of *jury*, a furnishing the verdict on which feeling, as the judge, must pass its sentence. This opinion, which has almost been taken by many for an axiom, I have assigned such reasons for calling in question, as I trust will procure its being reconsidered by its supporters. In opposing it, indeed, I am neither singular, nor without the aid of great names. But it appears to me that those on whose side I rank myself, have never taken the ground they were entitled to occupy, or, so to speak, come to sufficiently close quarters with their opponents. It seems to me, also, that the settlement of the question affects *the foundations of moral obligation* in a greater degree than is generally supposed; and that, in this point of view, it has never received all the attention it deserves.

Still it is inferior, at least in practical importance, to the question which relates to the final test or criterion of moral right and wrong; and to the latter question, accordingly, I have given a wider consideration. In this part of the subject, I have necessarily had occasion to review the

famous controversy about *Utility*; and I presume
to have defined, with more care and minuteness
than I am aware of having yet been employed,
the precise line which ought to divide the con-
tested ground. This line seems to me often to
take a different direction from what either the advocates or the opponents of the doctrine have assigned to it: the former at once claiming too much,
and receiving too little. While treating of this
question, I have gratified alike my love of truth,
and my love of justice, in endeavouring to rescue
the philosophical character of Paley from much
undeserved and indiscriminate obloquy. I say
indiscriminate, because while I admit the erroneous-
ness—even to absurdity—of some opinions uttered
by Paley, I consider his development of the nature and uses of general rules in morals, as the
most important contribution the science ever received from an individual. Any theoretical errors
that Paley may have fallen into, really belong to
a distinct part of the subject from that which it
forms his main object to consider. They are only
such errors as it would be, in a map of France, to
assign a wrong position to some frontier town in
Switzerland or *Belgium*, which the shape of the

map necessarily included. — If Paley has erred in his practical rules, he errs merely by reasoning inconsequentially from his own principles.

In proposing to offer this work to the public, I have been warned of the strong disrelish entertained, in the present state of taste, against whatever bears, or may have imputed to it, the character of *metaphysics*. This makes me desirous to say in what sense the work is, or is not, metaphysical. — If, by metaphysical, is meant (what most people understand by the term) dark — mystical — visionary — then I can assure the reader that he will find no more metaphysics in the book, than there is in this preface. No one can entertain a greater contempt than I do for some of the subjects to which the name of metaphysics is reckoned more peculiarly applicable, and for certain styles of writing, whose superabundance of obscurity is thought to make up for the deficiency of their other claims to that appellation. I have never attempted to pass off for an original idea, what is merely an unheard-of combination of words — or to make the reader believe, by merely *hiding myself* from him, that I am able to go farther into the subject than he is able to keep sight of me. Two aims I have pursued above all others—to obtain clear ideas myself;—to convey them clearly to others. To *clear* the subject—to clear it of doubt, perplexity, obscurity—was my whole design. But, for the very purpose of making it clear, it was necessary at times to employ a degree of closeness and precision of reasoning, and a minuteness of analysis, which may certainly require a little more attention than the pages of a novel or—(I was going to say a *poem*—but that modern poetry is, to me, the most hard to be understood of all species of writing.)—Purposes of mere perspicuity and precision, too, have dictated the occasional employment of words and terms appropriated more exclusively to philosophical uses, and which may not be absolutely familiar to a general reader. I have always adopted, indeed, the most *exact* way that occurred to me of expressing my meaning— so that the language is, at one time, technical and scholastic; at another, colloquial, it may be, to vulgarity. It is told of Buchanan that, when asked why he had made his pupil, King James, a *pedant*, he answered—it was doing a great deal to make any thing at all of him.—I must confess, that so great have I found the difficulties of the present subject, that I shall think I have done a great deal if I have been able to illustrate it *by any treatment, or in any language.*

There is, in the present age, a great and laudable desire to make every species of knowledge *generally accessible.* That theoretical morality has both interest and use enough for this purpose, I cannot doubt; but this I must say that its truths are not *yet* sufficiently clear and undisputed. The time for making short and smooth roads to this branch of knowledge is not yet come. We are, at present, little more than *surveying* the lines through which they are to pass.

Some persons who are great advocates for what they call plain and practical views of a subject, are in the frequent habit of coolly assuming as principles what is matter of great, and, it may be, very nice dispute. Such nice disputes may be termed useless, in the same sense that the foundation of a house is useless : — useless by itself, and for any of the actual purposes of a house, (the shelter and accommodation of the occupier,) for assuredly the foundation answers no such purposes. Nevertheless, to obtain this foundation, we must often *dig deep:* to the examination of the foundation, too, we must often resort to remedy cracks and flaws in the superincumbent masonry.

Even were the investigation of the principles of moral science less useful and interesting than it is in itself, there is nothing that more tends to the improvement of the *reasoning* powers. The indisposition of the present age to such exercises, is well seen in the looseness and irregularity of reasoning so often displayed in managing the topics of the day. It has often been said, that logic is only of use for exposing error, not for discovering truth. It would be nearly as good sense to say that the cords and pulleys are of use to draw up the curtain in a theatre, but not to discover the stage. What, in ninety-nine cases out of a hundred, where reasoning is employed, is the detection of error *but* the discovery of truth? Truth is seldom invisible so much either from the distance of the object, or the deficiency of our optics, as from the clouds of error with which it has been enveloped. Disperse these, and truth stands plain before you. For the detection of error, if the use of logic is not now, it will, I think, at a future time, be perceived. The prejudice against the cultivation of this science, founded on the absurdities of the school-men, is much about as reasonable as would be a like prejudice against modern chemistry or astronomy, on account of the fooleries of the alchemists and astrologers.

After all, however, the subject of ethical philosophy lies somewhere between the *metaphysical* and the *popular;* and I am able to name *one* work on this subject, which is one of the most *entertaining* books in the language — I allude to Dr. Adam Smith's *Theory of Moral Sentiments.* It is generally allowed, however, that its value, as a *theory,* bears but a small proportion to that which belongs to it as a magazine of facts and observations, and as a tasteful composition ; and but little penetration is required to discover the flimsiness and looseness of the frame-work, on which has been suspended such a profusion of beautiful decorations.—It is but giving the present work its due chance of success to say, that much of it is decidedly of a popular character* — the metaphysi-

---

* As of this cast, may be mentioned the whole of Part V., which — by the way — contains a speculation on the nature of certain mental qualities (of a kind between the moral and intellectual) and the regards excited by them, which seem to have been but little attended to.

cal portions, indeed, are so occasional as almost to admit of being particularized.

In the contrast between the intricacy and difficulty of a theoretical, and the interest of a popular or didactic delineation of the nature of virtue and vice, I have often been struck with the resemblance to the case of *music* — so complex and abstruse as a science, so delightful as an art; or, if I may use another comparison which I have somewhere seen employed, for this, or a similar purpose,—I should say that the theoretical bears the same relation to the descriptive or sentimental moralist, that the anatomist does to the painter or the sculptor. To the latter the object of study is the graces of form, of attitude, of motion: the former has to penetrate with his knife into the dark recesses of the animal frame, and to exhibit the machinery of bones, and muscles, and tubes, and vessels, which support the structure of external beauty, and effect the motions of external grace.

CONTENTS

OF

THE FIRST VOLUME.

PART I.

OF THE SUBJECTS, GENERALLY, OF A THEORY OF MORALS, AND OF THE NATURE OF THE MORAL FACULTY.

Page

CHAPTER I. — Principal divisions of the inquiry. -   1

CHAPTER II. — Of specific distinctions comprehended in the general term (morally) *good* — Objections to Dr. T. Brown's account of the notion of an *action in morals.* -   -   -   4

CHAPTER III. — On the question whether the perception of moral distinctions resolves ultimately into a judgment of reason or into an emotion.

SECTION I. — Positive argument that Reason perceives a moral distinction in actions. -   -   23

SECTION II. — Absurdity of the consequences that flow from the hypothesis that approbation and disapprobation are mere emotions. — Examination of Dr. Hutcheson's and Dr. Brown's defences. -   -   -   -   -   -   -   39

Page

SECTION III.—Inadequacy of the supposition that approbation and disapprobation are mere emotions, to explain the phenomena of our moral sentiments. — Exemplification from the statements of Dr. Brown and Dr. Smith.   -   -   -   58

APPENDIX TO SECT. III.—Of the nature of our dependence on the constancy of the laws of nature.   -   -   -   -   -   -   -   89

SECTION IV.—Of positive arguments against the supposition that *Reason* judges of moral distinctions.   -   -   -   -   -   -   94

APPENDIX TO CHAP. III.—Remarks on Sir James Mackintosh's " Preliminary Dissertation" in the new edition of the Encyclopædia Britannica. -   -   -   -   -   -   111

CHAPTER IV.—View of the origin and nature of our moral judgments and feelings, and of the related principles of action.

SECTION I.—Of judgments and feelings strictly moral.   -   -   -   -   -   -   -   134

SECTION II.—Of the natural affections.   -   -   152

SECTION III.—Of the precise sense in which approbation and disapprobation are acts of Reason.   162

CHAPTER V.—Recapitulation—analysis of the complex notion of a moral action.   -   -   172

CHAPTER VI.—Of the distinctive nature of the truths of moral science.

SECTION I.—Separation of certain inquiries occasionally confounded.   -   -   -   -   177

SECTION II.—Parallel between moral and mathematical truths.   -   -   -   -   -   -   187

PART II.

DOCTRINES OF THE SCIENCE OF MORALS.

Page

CHAPTER I. — Moral axioms, or first principles of moral truth. - - - - - 195

CHAPTER II. — Of the moral *fitness* of certain *ends* or *effects*. - - - - - 207

CHAPTER III. — Of *obligation* or *duty* as lying upon an *agent*.

SECTION I. — Of *general* obligations—as arising from the proper and immediate effects of actions—Theory of the construction of moral rules. - 213

SECTION II. — Of *special* obligations—as arising from the circumstantial and derived effects of actions—Source of the obligation of a promise—gratitude —relationship.—Of distributive justice—rights and injuries. - - - - - - 247

CHAPTER IV. — Theory of civil government — origin of political powers and rights. - - 270

CHAPTER V. — Theory of property. Nature of right acquired by possession—by labour. - 299

ERRATA.

VOL. I.

Page xiii   line 2 (Preface) for *a*, read *as*.
   19   ,,   5 for *something*, read *something's*.
   51   ,,   2 insert a *comma* after *virtue*.
   79   ,,   7 (from the bottom) read *we* as *in italics*, instead of the same word in the preceding line.
  149   ,,   6 for *in*, read *on*.
  238   ,,   14 insert a *comma* after *if*.

VOL. II.

    6   ,,   2 *close* the *parenthesis* with the word *be*.
  107   ,,   2 (from the bottom) cancel *comma* after desert.
       ,,   in last line, substitute *comma* for *semicolon* after *justice*.

PART I.

OF THE SUBJECTS, GENERALLY, OF A THEORY OF MORALS, AND OF THE NATURE OF THE MORAL FACULTY.

CHAPTER I.

INTRODUCTION. — PRINCIPAL DIVISIONS OF THE INQUIRY.

THE subjects of investigation in a *theory of morals* have generally been stated in two questions to the following effect.

First. By what faculty or principle of our mental constitution is it, that we perceive a *moral* distinction in characters and actions,—that we approve of one person or act, disapprove of another,—determine one to be good or right, another to be bad or wrong? Is it an independent power or capacity, essentially distinct from any other with which mind is endowed, and adapted to a specific purpose of its own,— or is it resolvable into any other power or capacity, which is therefore to be viewed as, in this respect, merely exercising itself after one specific mode, or on one particular class of its objects?

Secondly. It being, at all events, the *fact* that we have a perception of such distinctions, do the characters or actions that are thus distinguished as good or bad respectively, possess any assignable quality in common, more than that of being so distinguished—any quality *on account of which* it is that they are so distinguished,—and if so, what is that common quality?—wherein, as regards the actions themselves, does a good action differ from a bad or an indifferent one? what is the *object* of approbation in one action, of disapprobation in another? *For what* is one approved, another disapproved?

To the mode of treatment which the first of these questions has generally received, it may be objected, that such treatment has proceeded too much upon an assumption of the simplicity and uniformity of that operation or state of the mind to which the question refers, and which we designate by the term *approbation* or *disapprobation.*

To the mode of treatment generally pursued in regard to the second question it is in like manner to be objected, that, apparently, according to that mode, only one moral distinction has been supposed to exist, as applicable to characters and actions, namely, that denoted by the general terms good, right, meritorious, on the one hand, or bad, wrong, blameable, on the other; these terms or others similar being, in each case respectively, taken as synonymous.

If we carefully analyze into its several parts that act or state of the mind which we understand to be denoted by the term approbation or its contrary; that is, if we consider what approbation, in its common meaning, consists of, or comprehends; and if, at the same time, we accurately discriminate the different senses in which an action is denominated a good, or a bad one, we shall find we have done much to disentangle the perplexities that have usually beset this certainly very difficult subject.

CHAPTER II.

OF SPECIFIC DISTINCTIONS COMPREHENDED IN THE GENERAL
TERM (MORALLY) *GOOD*.

IF *approbation* means the perception or feeling that an action is good, and if there are more ways than one in which an action may be reckoned good, then approbation cannot, in every case, be an exercise of the moral faculty in one simple and uniform mode. According to the number of ways in which different actions, or the same action at once, may be *good*, the act of approbation must, in this respect if in no other, be proportionally varied or complex. Before considering, then, the nature of the moral faculty, it may be proper to advert to some of the principal distinctions about which it is conversant : these being, as will appear, more than the mere general one of *good* and *bad.*

An action is a *good* or approved one for this, if for nothing else, that it promotes the comfort or enjoyment of any sentient being. In the greater degree or to the greater extent it produces such an effect, it is even on this account alone so much a *better* action. It is a good action by which food is given to one that is suffering the want of it. It is a better action by which both food and clothing are given to one who is at once destitute of both. It is a good action by which one indigent person is relieved ; it is a better action by which two, or five, or twenty are relieved.

But, of two actions, each producing the same amount of good, if one is performed by an agent solely for the sake of, or with a view to the production of good, the other without any such view, — though both actions would be equally good in the sense just given, the latter one would, in another sense, not be a good action in like manner as the former. But in so far as it might proceed partly from a wish on the part of the agent to effect the good, partly from other and different motives, it would so far be a better action than one performed without any view at all to the production of good. And the more anxious an agent were to perform a beneficent action, if his eagerness were so great as to make him entirely overlook the prejudice or disadvantage which the performance of it might occasion to himself, we should pronounce his action to be so much a better action.

Yet again, if another agent, though also disposed to perform a beneficent action on its own account, nevertheless experienced much hesitation and reluctance about incurring the necessary sacrifice, and at last only by doing violence to his own inclination prevailed on himself to pursue the generous line of conduct, we should certainly say that the action of this person was a good action, in a sense in which that of the other was not. Though the action was less good on account of the reluctance felt in performing it, yet it was better on account of the effort made to overcome that reluctance; and which, but for such reluctance, could not have been exhibited.

In the first case, then, the greatness of the benefit done is made the measure of the goodness of the action; in the second, the degree in which the agent was moved by the desire of doing good to the exclusion of other motives; in the third, the greatness of the effort employed to supply the want of such desire, or to overcome opposing desires.

In the first description of cases too, let it be observed, that the omission of the better or more approved action would be the more disapproved; in the second and third cases, the omission of the better or more approved action would be the less disapproved.

If means have alike existed by which an inconsiderable, and by which an extensive good might have been promoted, we feel more disapprobation on account of the latter's being missed, than of the former's being so; on the other hand, that a man has not shewn a little desire or not made a slight effort to do good, is what we disapprove of more, than that he has not shewn a great desire, or made a great effort.

Yet there is another case, in which one action may be better than another, for reasons different from any of those assigned in the three preceding instances ; or where, at least, the *omission* of the one, would be more *disapproved* than that of the other : and this on account of certain peculiar circumstances of relation subsisting between the agent, and the person affected by the action. If I have received a benefit from another person, it may be a better action, one that would be more approved, to perform some act of beneficence towards him, than towards another person to whom the same favour might be of greater value. Nor would the former act cease to be better or more approved than the latter, in the sense now used, although the latter should be performed with the most benevolent intentions, and should also furnish occasion for much heroism and self-denial.

In the first of the senses now described, an action is good or fit ; in the second, it is good or virtuous ; in the third, good or meritorious ; in the fourth, good or (specially) obligatory.

An action cannot be obligatory without being fit, and vice versa ; but it is not necessarily obligatory in the proportion that it is fit,* (i.e. fit in the

---

* It will afterwards be shown that obligation must, in every instance whatever, arise from the fitness or unfitness of some *effect*, and cannot possibly arise or exist otherwise. But I have wished in the meantime to let it appear clearly, that the obligation to perform an action is by no means according to

sense of positively useful or beneficial;) an action cannot be meritorious without being virtuous,* but may be virtuous without being meritorious. It may be both virtuous and meritorious, and not obligatory.

The proportion in which an action possesses any one of these qualities, may have no correspondence with that in which it possesses another. To save the life of twenty persons is a better action (more *fit*) than to save the life of one. To save the life of one, may be a better (more *virtuous*) action than to save the life of twenty: it may be performed more exclusively from motives of duty,— under circumstances evincing a greater regard to duty. If regard to duty is so strong as at once to overcome all opposing motives of ease or safety, the action is better (more *virtuous*) than in a case of a different kind, where these opposing motives must be overcome by a strong mental effort: yet in the latter case again, the action is better (more *meritorious*) than when the regard to duty spontaneously prevailed. To pay a shilling that I owe to a neighbour, is a better action (more *obligatory*) than to distribute five pounds among the poor: yet to distribute a considerable sum among the poor, is better (more *fit*) than to pay

the fitness of the positive or proper effects of that action, or its beneficial consequences; and at all events it still remains true, that our notions of *fitness* and *obligation* are not the same.

* i. e. Virtuous in kind, however little in degree.

a trifle to one who has perhaps little use for it. Either of these two actions again may, in other senses, be better (more *virtuous*, more *meritorious*) than the other.

It is very evident then that the general terms expressive of a moral quality, such as *good* or *approvable*, are used in a variety of senses; and that the more specific terms which these may comprehend or denote, are by no means of inter-changeable application. Thus we have seen that though disapprobation is, in a general sense, the opposite of approbation, yet the omission of an approved action is sometimes the more disapproved that the action would have been more approved, sometimes the less disapproved on that account; also that an action that is the most fit, may not be by any means the most virtuous, the most merito-rious, or the most obligatory; that an action may be highly obligatory, fit in a very trifling degree, and not at all virtuous or meritorious; yet the epithet *good* or *approvable* may be applied to it, to denote the degree in which it possesses any one, or all of these attributes.

If an action may thus, in different ways, be, at the same time, better than another action, and not so good as that other, surely we shall inquire in vain for a single common quality that will consti-tute its goodness.

Nor could it, with propriety, be said, that each of these are merely different species of goodness, that might be combined together so as to form a greater amount of that quality; that for instance an action possessing two of the qualities enumerated, would therefore possess a greater amount or degree of goodness than an action possessed of only one of them, just as a man that has both landed property and money in the funds, is a richer man than if he had only one of these. The moral attributes described are really, so to speak, not of the same genus; they are not the attributes of the same subject; they are at least as different from one another, as the figure of a body is from its size, its situation in place, or its existence in time.

On these distinctions, which will yet be farther pursued and illustrated, I have now to observe, that some of them, (such as that between fitness and obligation, and that between virtue and merit,) seem to have almost or altogether escaped the attention of moral theorists; that, in general, the difference between the notions expressed respectively by the terms fitness, obligation, &c. have been but very imperfectly understood and vaguely stated; and that even in respect of the degree in which such distinctions may have actually been recognized, they have nevertheless been almost entirely lost sight of in many of the controversies that have occurred in relation to the theory of morals: and philosophers have gone on enquiring what makes one action good, another bad, as

if these two terms, or others synonymous, expressed all the distinctions about which our moral powers are conversant.

But I have never met with more than one instance, in which the reality of these distinctions
has been fairly called in question. The doctrine
which has lately been maintained on this head is
so extraordinary in itself, and has been urged by
authority so powerful, that it requires the fullest
consideration.

The late Dr. Thomas Brown, in the system of
ethics which forms a part of his university lec-
tures, lays it down as a fundamental point to be
carefully held in view throughout the whole en-
quiry, that "an action in morals, is nothing but
the agent acting." He accordingly insists upon
an entire rejection of the common distinction between the goodness of the agent and that of the
act : asserting that it is impossible for an agent to
be good, an action bad, or *vice versa*. " When we
speak of an action," he observes, " as virtuous,
without regard to the merit of the particular agent,
we only conceive some other agent acting in
different circumstances, and exciting in us, consequently, a different feeling of approbation, by
the difference of the frame of mind which we
suppose ourselves to contemplate;" — which is to
say, if I rightly understand Dr. Brown's meaning,
that when a man, intending to do evil, actually
does good — if we call the man bad, the action

good, we merely mean that another agent who should perform the same action, intending it to produce good, would be a good agent. Well; but does it not remain true, even in this way of stating the matter, that there is one sort of *effect*, which if an agent intends to produce, he will be a good agent; another sort of effect which if an agent intends to produce, he will be a bad agent? These different sorts of effects then must have different names; the one must be called a good, the other a bad effect; or they must be distin- guished in some other way. Now the *action*, strictly so called, is just as distinct from the *intention* of the agent, as it is from the *effect* pro- duced; and in the manner in which it stands re- lated to each, may as justly be characterized from the nature of the one, as from that of the other. If, compassionating the distress and terror of a prisoner, I set him at liberty, the *action* is merely the motion of my hand which turns the key of his dungeon, or looses his chain. That *action*, taken by itself, is no more capable of hav- ing a moral character applied to it than the twirl- ing of my watch chain, or the flapping of my handkerchief. But as, on the one hand, the *ac- tion* supposed is performed with a certain *intention*, so, on the other, the performance is attended with a certain *effect*; and surely Dr. Brown would have allowed that the *effect* may be good while the *intention* is bad, or *vice versa*. Thus, in the case supposed, my intention of relieving the prisoner is good; the effect of letting him escape from punishment and setting him loose to do more mischief — is bad. Now whether or not the *action* (which, as I have said, stands *between* the intention and the effect — being equally distinct from, and equally related to each — but which must take all its *moral* character from the one or from the other) — whether or not the action, when spoken of as morally good or bad, is to be spoken of *only* in conjunction with the intention — (for this is all that can be meant by saying that an action in morals is only the agent acting) — is a dispute relating entirely to a verbal matter. The substantial point is this — is an *effect*, or an effect and the action producing it, — abstractedly from any intention of the agent — capable of being the subject of a *moral determination?* Is any effect what *ought* to be, any other effect what *ought not* to be? are we morally pleased or satisfied with one effect, and the action producing it — morally displeased or dissatisfied with another effect, and the action producing it — irrespectively of any intention on the part of an agent? This point I refer to Dr. Brown himself.

" When we speak," says he, " of an action as virtuous, we speak of it as separated from all those accidental intermixtures of circumstances which may cloud the discrimination of an individual; when we speak of a person as virtuous, we speak of him as acting perhaps under the influence of such accidental circumstances : and though his action, considered as an action which might have been performed by any man under the influence of other circumstances, may excite our moral disapprobation in a very high degree, our disapprobation is not extended to him. The emotion which he excites is pity, not any modification of dislike. We wish he had been better informed ; and when his general conduct has impressed us favourably, we feel perfect confidence that in the present instance also, if he had been better informed, he would have acted otherwise."

Now what, I would ask, can be meant by speaking of the " discrimination of an individual" as " clouded," by " pitying" him, or by " wishing that he had been better informed :" what is the use, in short, of all the practical rules of morality, if " an action in morals is only the agent acting ?" If an action, merely flowing from good intentions, is right in all the senses in which an action can be right, and if it is impossible for what is done to be wrong, if what is intended be right; surely an agent who intends well, cannot be mistaken in his consciousness of the nature of his intention; and if he cannot be mistaken in this particular, he cannot, according to Dr. Brown, be mistaken in any thing at all affecting the moral character of the action : why then pity him, or wish he had been

better informed? Even on the author's own show-
ing, then, there is something more that we desire
in an action, than merely the good intentions of
the agent. If we must not, according to **Dr.**
Brown, denominate this the goodness of the action, we must just have some other name for it:
and this, so far as I am able to gather, is the
total result that flows from the establishment of
Dr. Brown's favourite position, that " an action in
morals is only the agent acting." Indeed we may
lay our account with finding that, whenever an
author sets himself to contradict a sentiment that
is universally understood and assented to, such as
this, that a man with good intentions may commit
a wrong action, he involves us in a mere question
of words.

If a man were, by fraud or violence, to maintain
possession of a property which ought to belong to
another, it would, I apprehend, be a very intelligible and convenient method of stating the nature
of such a case, to say, " the one is proprietor in
point of right, the other in point of fact." **Now**
suppose any one were to tell us that this is quite a
superfluous and imaginary distinction, tending to
nothing else but to perplex and obscure our notions of property; that there is really no such
thing as being a proprietor in fact only; that the
proprietor is, and only can be, he who has the
right of possession; and that when we speak of
any one as being proprietor in fact, as opposed

to being so in right, we merely speak of what such a one would be under a different situation of circumstances; that is, what he would be if he were in possession by right.   Is it possible to imagine greater trifling than this? yet the results here obtained exhibit, in a different instance, all that Dr. Brown accomplishes by his rejection of the common distinction between the goodness of an action, and the goodness of an agent.

Perhaps it may be said, our disappointment in such cases as those spoken of in the last extract from Dr. B. is still conceived wholly in relation to the agent; and that his ignorance, or want of capacity, implied in his mistake of the means to fulfil his intentions, though they are not morally wrong, yet indicate deficiency and imperfection. Now it is undeniable that our estimation of the agent is, in a certain way, increased or lessened, according as he is more or less capable of contriving means to an end, or powerful in employing them.   But it is no less undeniable, that our opinion of an agent suffers as much *in this respect* from a view of his incapacity or inability to compass a bad end as a good one.   But as, when an agent, meaning to do good, actually does evil, our respect for the purity of his intention does not prevent us from at once despising his incapacity and sincerely regretting the event; so when a man meaning to do evil, actually does good, our reprobation of his purpose and contempt of his incapacity (as in the other case) do not prevent us from being sincerely rejoiced at his failure.

An action then, as restricted by Dr. Brown to mean the *person acting with a certain intention,*— and even if we comprehend with the intention the skill and power displayed in fulfilling that intention,— an action, I say, even in this extended sense, is not the sole object of moral approbation or disapprobation. An action, as meaning the *person acting, and the effect produced by his acting,* is, by itself, the object of a moral sentiment. The thing done, as well as the person doing; the effect, as well as the intention, is that in which our moral faculties, whatever they may be, discover a good and a bad. We value the good intentions of the agent, even without reference to the end; but we also value the end, without reference to the good intentions of the agent; we value the wise adaptation of the means with reference to both; we admire the wisdom of the agent in adapting the means to the end; but we have also a distinct satisfaction with this adaptation, solely for the sake of the end. Though the sentiments excited by the agent, and those by the end, are of very different kinds, we bestow the name of approbation, or the contrary, on both, and apply indifferently to both agent and end several of the terms distinctive of moral qualities. We speak of approving an agent, approving an end, a good agent, a good end. The specific difference, however, be-

tween these qualities, when separately applied to
agents and ends, is also indicated by certain more
appropriate and exclusive designations; we speak
of a right or proper end, not of a right or proper
agent; an agent is virtuous, an end is not.

But I must maintain, farther, not merely that
there is a right and a wrong in ends, as separate
from that which is ascribed to intentions, but that
the former is the original and primary notion; the
other, which relates to intentions, being founded
upon it. That any supposed being, A. for instance,
should be happy rather than miserable, (i. e. that
it is fit, or right he should be so,) is a moral truth
of itself, perceived to be such independently of all
consideration of the goodness or badness of any
intention whatever; on the contrary, that the intention of B. to make A. happy, is good or right, is
not an original truth, but one which presupposes
a fitness in the effect which B. intends to produce;
nor can we possibly denominate any intention
good, without the supposition of such an antecedent fitness in the end as now described. If no
end were originally and in itself better than another, we should not understand what the good or
bad intentions of an agent meant. How could a
man be said to intend well or ill, if we knew of
nothing but those very intentions themselves,
which could be said to be good or bad? To use
an illustration that may here strike more than one
of a higher kind,—when we say that a man's coat

ought to fit him, or that we approve of its being made to fit him, do we mean by this merely that we shall approve the intentions of the tailor who makes it so? Surely any propriety in the intentions of the tailor can only exist in consequence of something being previously proper for him to intend.

The goodness of an end then does not consist in this, that it corresponds with the intentions of a good agent; but the goodness of an agent consists in this, that he wills or intends a good end. In order to know what is a good end, we do not enquire if it is what a good agent would pursue, but to know a good agent, we consider if the end he pursues is good.

Dr. Brown, after having represented the intentions or volitions of the agent as being alone that which can give birth to moral notions, proceeds in the work of simplification by maintaining the extraordinary position, that the virtue, merit, and obligation of an action, are precisely the same thing; that they are merely different names attached to the same quality, according as we view the action before, during, or after the time of its performance: it is obligatory before it is done, virtuous while it is in the course of being done, meritorious after it is done. — If it is at all necessary to a refute a doctrine so obviously untenable, I would remark that if the virtue, merit, and obligation of an action, have a reference merely to the point of time at which it is conceived, these qualities must, in every action, exist in the same degree; that is, in whatever proportion one action is more or less virtuous than another, it must likewise be more or less obligatory, more or less meritorious; it can never have more of one quality than of another; (for this would be equivalent to allowing that an action which was good or right before performance, might be better or worse after performance.) Now this is so far from being the case, that in some respects the very contrary is the case; for instance, the obligation and the merit of an action are generally in inverse proportion. I am under a strong obligation to pay for what I purchase, nobody will say I have any great merit in doing so. It is very obligatory not to rob or murder our neighbour, surely it is not also very meritorious; or else most people possess a stock of merit they little dream of. Howard had the very highest merit in visiting the prisons —the obligation was of the slightest kind. Let it be observed too, that all this holds good even if we admit with Dr. B. that an action in morals is only the agent acting, and that there is no distinction between the goodness of the agent and that of the act. For, even in the apprehension of the agent himself, and of those who concur with him in his estimate (just or not) of his duty, he is conceived (setting aside too all consideration of extrinsic circumstances affecting the ease or difficulty of performance) to have so much less merit as he only fulfils a so much greater, *and just because a greater*, obligation, and *vice versa*. Nor does it make the smallest difference to the perception, in this case, whether the action is contemplated before, during, or after its performance. We determine the relative proportion between the obligation and the merit quite alike at any of these points of time. The only visible foundation Dr. Brown's doctrine on this head possesses, is this, that an action cannot be obligatory after performance, nor meritorious before it. But surely this does not explain all that is meant by those two terms.

Dr. Brown complains that the theory of morals has been perplexed with unnecessary distinctions. But while I allow that some phenomena naturally the same, have been erroneously distributed into different classes, I do not despair of making it appear, that the chief difficulties that have embarrassed the subject in question, have arisen, not from this cause, but from one the very opposite of it: that is, partly because some important distinctions have, in a great measure, escaped the observation of inquirers; but still more, as I believe, because other distinctions that have been fully recognized and allowed, have not been held in view with the requisite steadiness, in the management of a variety of discussions, where the difficulties that occurred admitted of complete removal, by a simple reference to these distinctions.

Such a general idea as I have now attempted to furnish, of the different *sorts* of determinations that may be ascribed to the moral faculty, seems to me essential as a preparation for entering on the inquiry what that faculty is — so that we may be enabled to ascertain how far any of the different theories that have been advanced on this subject, are either altogether or exclusively true.

CHAPTER III.

ON THE QUESTION WHETHER THE PERCEPTION OF MORAL DIS-
TINCTIONS RESOLVES ULTIMATELY INTO A JUDGMENT OF
REASON OR INTO AN EMOTION.

SECT. I.

*Positive Argument that Reason perceives a Moral Distinction
in Actions.*

THE two great divisions of opinion in regard to
the nature of the moral faculty, of that, namely,
by which we perceive a moral distinction in characters and actions, may be thus described.

By some it has been maintained that, in the
constitution of our nature, a certain feeling or
emotion of an agreeable kind has been connected
with the contemplation of some actions, an emotion of an opposite, or disagreeable kind, with the
contemplation of others; that actions of the first
kind we call *good,* of the second kind *bad;* that
when we say of any action it is right, or obligatory,—what should be, or ought to be performed,—
what there would be virtue or merit in performing, —what an agent would deserve commenda-

tion or reward for performing,—we mean just this, that the action in question, or at most that all actions distinguished by some particular quality belonging to that action, are such as we are formed to behold with an agreeable emotion, and we mean nothing else whatever. This opinion has been supported by Dr. Hutcheson, Mr. Hume, Dr. Adam Smith, and, more latterly, by Dr. Thomas Brown.

Of these, Dr. Smith alone has attempted to resolve the capacity of moral emotion into another principle of our nature, namely, that of sympathy. By all the rest of these philosophers, the moral faculty is represented as an original and elementary part of our constitution.*

By another class of theorists, forming the second great division, it has been maintained, that the mere agreeable or disagreeable emotion experienced by the spectator at the view of an action, cannot be all that characterises that action as good or bad; since these distinctions express something belonging to actions absolutely, and independently of what emotions the view of them may excite; that certain actions are right, whether they should please any being or not; and that if, from being so constituted as to experience a disagreeable emotion at the view of such actions,

* Hartley has also conceived that the moral faculty may be resolved into a more general principle, namely, that of association.

any being should determine them to be wrong, he would determine falsely. This has been the view of Clarke, Cudworth, Price, Butler, Reid, and Stewart.

So far the opinion of these philosophers is but negatively described. The three first named however, viz. Clarke, Cudworth, and Price, have represented the moral faculty as being the same with that by which, in other cases, we distinguish between truth and falsehood, namely,—reason or the understanding. If Butler, Reid, and Stewart have not asserted this, or have even denied it, they have at least offered no arguments in support of such denial. — A difficulty which I feel in more explicitly classing their views, will afterwards be adverted to.

It is somewhat singular that the term *moral sense*, which originated from among the first division of theorists above enumerated, (namely from Dr. Hutcheson,) has been objected to by some of those, while it has been defended by some of the partisans of the other system of opinions. Thus, on the one hand, Dr. Smith and Dr. Brown would discard the use of that phrase, while, on the other, Dr. Reid and Mr. Stewart seem disposed to retain it. To put the question then, as is not unfrequently done, whether we perceive moral distinctions by reason or by a sense, would not, without carefully restricting the import of the latter term, necessarily be to present a statement either of more general differences, or of the special points on which those differences hang suspended. What those points are, as distinct from those on which there is an agreement, has never, I think, been satisfactorily laid down; or, to speak more correctly, there would seem to be no understood basis, no admitted principles, upon which the controversy might be brought to a decision.

After an attentive consideration of the arguments employed on each side of the debate, I cannot find that parties are agreed on any one of the following points :—

First. Whether there are any moral propositions (by which I mean, propositions affirming some actions to be right, others wrong) that are immutably, or even absolutely true; that is, true in such a manner, that if any one were to assert the contrary of such propositions, he would assert what is false — or false otherwise than in reference to the present actual constitution of the human mind?

Secondly. Whether the *admission* that there are certain immutable or absolute truths in morals, is sufficient effectually to negative the supposition that approbation and disapprobation are mere emotions?

Or, Thirdly. Whether the admission that certain moral truths are immutable (with or without the additional admission that our perception of these truths cannot resolve into a mere emotion,) necessarily obliges us to resort to *reason* as the faculty by which such truths are discovered ?*

To most persons I imagine it will appear, that, if these are really the points on which the controversy turns — and I am unable to discover that they can be different from these — the maintainance of it must have been owing, not to any difficulty in determining such points, but to some carelessness in distinguishing them, or some disinclination to discuss them, on the part of some or other of the different sets of disputants engaged.

With regard to the first point :—

That there is something in morality that is absolute and immutable, that there is something right which never could be wrong, something wrong which never could be right ; that the same actions which are right just now, must, if continuing in all respects the same, and performed under the same circumstances, be right at all times ; that to pronounce them wrong, would be false now, and always false, whatever might be the constitution, the feelings, or the judgment of the being who pronounced them so,—all this is what seems to me to lie absolutely beyond the reach of doubt or question.

---

* I should be inclined to represent Dr. Brown only as giving a negative to the first question — Dr. Hutcheson, Dr. Smith, and Sir James Mackintosh, an affirmative to the first, a negative to the second—Dr. Reid and Mr. Stewart an affirmative to the first and second ; but a negative to the third. Dr. Price gives an affirmative to all the three.

And in the next place, and in regard to the second point : —

If, when we pronounce an action to be right, it is admitted that we pronounce something that is *absolutely*, not to say immutably, *true of such action*, — then to affirm that, in thus pronouncing concerning the action, we mean only that the contemplation of it excites *in us* an agreeable emotion, seems to me an inconsistency of the most palpable nature.

An argument that has been used for the purpose of removing this inconsistency, (and which it is necessary to advert to, *in limine*,) is one which strikes entirely wide of the mark at which it aims.

We are told that, though in pronouncing an action to be right, we merely express an emotion felt by us, yet there is some absolute quality in the action which is proper to excite this emotion, and but for which the emotion would not arise; that consequently to say that we have the emotion, is to say something absolutely true of the action, namely, that the action has that absolute quality which excites the emotion.

Now in regard to this statement, I would only, at present, ask,—is the absolute quality which is here said to belong to the action (that quality by which the emotion is excited) is this quality the *moral goodness* or *rightness* of the action? If it is, then the action's being morally good or right, cannot merely imply that we have an agreeable emotion at the view of it; for the goodness of the action being supposed the quality which excites the emotion, must exist independently of that emotion. Surely it will not be said that the action is good, because the view of it affords us an agreeable emotion; and then that the emotion itself arises because the action is good.

On the other hand, if the *moral goodness* is not the quality which excites the emotion, the solution offered does not meet the difficulty. It is not enough to tell us, for instance, that the benevolence or the utility of an action is an absolute quality belonging to the action, and indicated by the emotion; the truth regarding the action which we are assuming, and yet assert, to be absolute, is, not that it is *benevolent* or *useful;* but, (supposing either benevolence or utility to be that *for* which it is determined to be morally good,) that a benevolent or a useful action, is *good* or *right.* In short, the absolute truth conveyed in affirming that we experience a particular emotion at the view of a particular sort of action, is not the absolute truth to which the present question relates, but another, and quite a different one.

Leaving however this, and all that regards the second point generally, as the subject of farther consideration in the sequel, I would now observe, in regard to the third point, that, if there are any absolute and immutable truths in morals, then no other faculty than that of reason itself would seem competent to pronounce them to be such; and that we are every way warranted in ascribing this function to reason, is what I shall now endeavour more fully to make appear.

First, as a specific instance of an absolute and immutable truth in morals, I would offer this single proposition — " The happiness of any being *ought* to be promoted by himself and others, rather than his misery." Take this proposition by itself, and irrespectively of all circumstances not therein stated, and, I would ask, is it *true?* Could the contrary of it be conceived to be true? Nay, could the proposition itself ever cease to be true? If any one should say that it ever might or could be *right*, for a being to seek to cause misery to himself or others, simply for the sake of doing so, (for I repeat, the proposition is to be taken irrespectively of all extrinsic circumstances) or that it ever might or could cease to be right for a being to promote happiness rather than misery, if both were equally possible, say even if he were under the necessity of doing one or other, with no reason whatever on either side, but what might be perceived in the nature of each,—for it matters not how abstractly, nakedly, or sparingly, or with what limitations or provisions the necessary truth of the proposition specified is admitted,—with such a one I should be unable to argue farther. I can conceive no greater absurdities to which I could, by reasoning, reduce the opinions of an opponent in debate.

But, if it is admitted that the proposition is true, and what cannot but be true, I would only farther ask, whether, in this case, it wants any of the characteristics of a self-evident necessary truth; and why it should, more than any other truth of that nature, be supposed to be discovered by any other faculty than reason?

It would certainly seem that those who deny the exercise of reason in this case, are bound either to produce an instance of an immutable truth that is not conceived to be discovered by reason, or to show that the immutable truths of morality want something that is observed to characterize those truths that are allowed to be discovered by reason.

Are there any truths at all perceived by reason? what are they? what do they possess that this one wants?

Let reference be made to the case of mathematical axioms. Take such instances as these, "all the parts are equal to the whole," — "things which are equal to the same are equal to one another." Why must we at once affirm that these propositions are true, and that the contrary of them cannot be true? Plainly for this, because what we affirm in each proposition, is involved in the very notion of that whereof we make the affirmation — the subject of the affirmation would cease to be what it is, were that not true which is affirmed of it. And is not this the case with those things which are the subjects of such moral propositions as have been instanced?   When we say of happiness, that it ought to be pursued and imparted, and of misery, that it ought to be avoided and prevented, do we not say something that is involved in the very notion of happiness and misery?   Would happiness continue to be happiness, if it ought to be avoided or withheld? Could we conceive a misery that ought to be pursued or inflicted, more than we could conceive a circle with unequal diameters, or a triangle with one side greater than the other two?   If the moral proposition then seems as necessarily and immutably true as the mathematical one; if our conviction of its necessary truth seems to arise in precisely the same manner, why ascribe that conviction to reason in the one case, to a different faculty in the other?

If any proposition can at all force itself upon our minds as an immutable and necessary truth, it cannot possibly be in any other way than that now described; namely, that what is affirmed in the proposition is so necessarily involved in our conception of the subject, that to deny or contradict the proposition would be absolutely to remove or destroy that conception.   On the other hand, I can for my own part form no other idea of what reason is, than simply of its being the faculty by which we perceive what any conception involves in it.   To say then that a proposition may be necessarily true, and yet not perceived to be true by reason, is, in my apprehension, a contradiction in terms.

It is needless to observe, that, if reason can determine any *moral proposition* to be *true*, reason must thence be reckoned, to that extent, a judge of moral distinctions.

Dr. Reid, though one of those who maintain the absolute nature of moral distinctions, has yet vindicated the supposition of a peculiar inward *sense*, as the faculty discriminating right and wrong, on the ground that our senses do not merely convey to us certain sensations, but assure us of certain qualities belonging to external objects, absolutely, and independently of our sensations, and which we must conceive as belonging to them, whatever our sensations might be. In this he has been followed by Mr. Dugald Stewart. But Dr. Reid's theory of external perception is, I apprehend, superseded by a more refined analysis ; and it seems abundantly clear, that not any one of our senses, by itself, could furnish us with the notion of a body externally subsisting, nor consequently with the notion of any of the primary qualities of matter : notions which are the result of a comparison of the reports of various senses. But, apart from this consideration, there is nothing that our senses can judge to be true or false of outward objects (admitting that the senses could form judgments) that at all resemble our moral judgments on actions. To judge that a body is square or round, is to judge of nothing but a fact, which might be otherwise ; to judge more generally that matter has figure, is impenetrable,—is not to assert anything of matter, previously conceived as the subject of a proposition ; because it is necessary to our conception of the subject. To say, on the other hand, that an action is right, is to assert something which cannot be otherwise ; while yet its being right, though involved in our conception of it, is not a part of that conception. Thus I perceive that to inflict gratuitous pain is a wrong action, and can never be a right one : yet my conception of the action itself, is complete without reference to its moral character.

But the fact is, moreover, that whatever truths regarding matter bear the least resemblance to moral truths, are really discovered, as well as these, by reason. Our ideas of the figure and impenetrability of matter, are conveyed to us through our senses ; they are the essential qualities of matter, which make it to be matter ; they are objects of knowledge, not of reason. But is this the case as regards the divisibility, the finite extension, and *vis inertiæ* of matter ? Are these objects of sense ? A dog discovers figure and impenetrability,—does he discover the attributes just named ? Or are they discovered by us, otherwise than by reason ? Thus then even in what relates to material objects, the qualities to which alone the moral qualities of

actions seem to bear any analogy, are not discovered by our senses, but by reason.

In truth, however, these remarks regard at most
but a question of words. The name of a *sense*
may, without any great impropriety, be given to
the moral faculty, simply as a discriminating faculty, and whatever may be its nature. To reason
itself we may give the name of a sense of truth
and falsehood. The question is not, whether we
discover moral distinctions by a *sense*, in this general meaning of the term ;* for this would import no

* On account of this ambiguity, some inconveniences arising
from which will afterwards appear, I should choose, if possible,
to avoid using the expression *moral sense ;* but if, to prevent
circumlocution, I may occasionally have recourse to it, it will
never be in the general, but in the limited sense, as denoting a
faculty distinct from reason, and a faculty which is nothing
more than a susceptibility of receiving agreeable or disagreeable emotions from the view of different actions. With this
definition of a moral sense, Dr. Reid and Mr. Stewart, though
allowing of the term, would be reckoned opposers of the doctrine. Dr. Brown, on the other hand, though averse to the
use of the term, would be reckoned a supporter of the doctrine.
It is by a reference to Dr. Reid's theory of external perception, that two parties, differing widely in opinion as to the
nature of the moral faculty, have each justified their employment of the term *moral sense.* When we behold a material
body, says Dr. Reid, we have a sensation (which is something
in us,) and a perception of something *in the body,* existing independently of our sensation. Now one party has assimilated
our moral determinations to the sensation, the other to the
perception. It is the former that I exclusively designate as
supporters of the *moral sense ;* and it is with them that my
quarrel more particularly, or even wholly lies.

more than to ask if we discerned right and wrong,
by a faculty discerning right and wrong. The
question is,—is the faculty commonly called reason
competent to discern moral distinctions, or any
moral distinctions at all ; or does the perception of
these distinctions require also another and different
faculty ? And those who maintain the negative of
the first question, and the affirmative of the second,
seem bound to prove, first, that there could exist a
being possessed of reason, who should yet be unable to distinguish right from wrong; and secondly,
that a being could possess the power of distinguishing right from wrong, and yet be destitute of reason :
— either of which propositions, I think, it would
require a metaphysician of some enterprize to
maintain.   Until such propositions are established,
it must be held as unphilosophical to assume the existence of any moral faculty separate from reason ;
and if the moral faculty be recognised as the same
with reason, it must tend to produce misapprehen-
sion and confusion to give it a distinct name.

This leads me to remark more generally upon
the manner on which the two eminent writers last
named (Dr. Reid and Mr. D. Stewart) have expressed themselves upon this subject. So far as
I am able to comprehend their opinions, I should
not be inclined to rank them among the number
of those who have ascribed our perception of
moral distinctions to reason ; since they appear at
most to own that the moral faculty (which, accord-

ing to them, is an original principle of our nature) may be comprehended with other faculties under the general name of reason. I cannot help considering this mode of representing the nature of the moral faculty as extremely unphilosophical, if it implies, and I see nothing else it can imply, that a being might exist, able to reason on other subjects, and yet not upon moral subjects; one who, for instance, on forming the conceptions of whole and parts, could perceive the necessary truth of this proposition, "the whole must be equal to all the parts," and thus form the notion of equality, — and who yet, though able to form the conceptions of happiness and misery, could not perceive the truth of this proposition, " the happiness of any being ought to be promoted, his misery not promoted," nor thus form the ideas of right and wrong. This seems to me as much as to say that there must be as many different original faculties, as there are subjects of thought or conception; that one faculty, for instance, perceives that a body cannot be in two places at once, another that space is infinite, a third that time is without beginning or end, and so on. But besides, Dr. Reid, if not Mr. Stewart also, does not hesitate to place the first principle of morals among the number of necessary truths. Now it seems to me that if we once admit more than one supreme judge of necessary truth, we abandon the unity of truth itself; and shall be compelled to entertain the supposition, that each of two contradictory propositions might be necessarily true: since it would be beyond our power to assure ourselves that principles of the different kinds might not, in their remoter consequences, come into hostile collision. We should place ourselves much in the situation of a country having two supreme courts of law, whose jurisdiction it might not be possible to keep asunder, while each should be entitled to enforce its own decisions.

But whatever question may be made regarding the name that is to be given to the faculty by which we distinguish between right and wrong — and how little the name determines the real controversy is evident from this, that reason admits of being called the moral sense, and the moral sense of being called a part of reason — there can, I think, be no question, if there is any thing immutable in right and wrong, that the moral faculty cannot be, in its nature, a mere susceptibility of emotion, varied according to the character of the different actions which we behold. I have, in this chapter, offered a specific proposition as one instance of the absolute and immutable nature of right and wrong; one instance, as I conceive, of our perception that there is something right, and something wrong, which can never be otherwise. Now if those distinctions entirely resolve into certain emotions experienced by us at the view of certain actions, these two propositions — "it is

right for a being to occasion misery to himself and
others," and, "the view of a being occasioning
misery to himself and others moves in us the
emotion of approbation,"* — would be equivalent
and identical. But if they are equivalent and
identical, then to say that the first can never be
true, would be to say that a certain emotion cannot
possibly be connected with, or made to follow the
view of a certain action; an affirmation which
would be plainly absurd : if they are not identical,
then the emotion felt by us, cannot be all that
distinguishes right from wrong. And this leads
me more particularly to consider, as in the following section, the absurd consequences that would
flow from the supposition that the peculiar emotion
with which an action is viewed, is that alone by
which its moral nature is distinguished.

SECT. II.

*Absurdity of the Consequences that flow from the Hypothesis
that Approbation and Disapprobation are mere Emotions.*

The supporters of the doctrine of a moral sense
seldom deign to vindicate that doctrine from the absurd consequences that have been attached to it;
nor, so far as I know, have even such vindications
as have been offered, ever met with that degree of
exposure to which their weakness lays them open.

* " To say that an action excites in us the feeling, and to
say that it appears to us right, are to say precisely the same
thing." — Dr. Thomas Brown, Lecture 74.

The fundamental objection to the doctrine of a moral sense is this, that, if, when we pronounce an agent or action morally good, we mean, simply, that the view of such action or agent excites in the spectator an agreeable emotion, then the affirmation that such action or agent is good, does not express any thing that is true of such *agent* or *action*, but only something that is true of the *spectator*, namely, that *he* is affected after a peculiar manner by the view of a particular action,— a consequence which cannot fail of being considered as sufficiently absurd.   Nor, as I have before shewn, is this consequence in the least to be obviated by telling us, (the accustomed fallacy to which the advocates of a moral sense resort,) that one action is *absolutely* of a certain quality the view of which affects us agreeably, that another action is absolutely of a certain quality the view of which affects us disagreeably.   These two propositions — the action is of a certain quality — the view of this quality affects us agreeably — do not just *mean one thing*. The question then is, which of the two, upon the hypothesis of a moral sense, is identical in meaning with this one — the action is *right*.   If the former, you give up your hypothesis itself; (in as much as you thereby own that the feeling is not what constitutes the action right, but is consequent on its being right ;) if the latter, you allow " it is right " to be synonymous with " we feel the agreeable emotion " — which leaves the objection in force.

Whatever absurdity then belongs to the representation that right and wrong mean nothing that is true of an agent or act, but only something that is true of a spectator,—whatever other absurdities may be connected with this one,—these absurdities are not in the slightest degree removed by shewing — in the sense in which the advocates of a moral sense do shew this — that, in asserting an action to be good, they assert something that is absolutely true of it. The absolute quality of which they assert—or rather of which their assertion supposes — the existence, is only the *subject* of the attribute, right or wrong, not that attribute itself. The attribute, as they explain wherein the attribute consists, is merely the feeling of the spectator, something that is true of him; and the absurdity imputable to the doctrine of a moral sense lies in the supposition (a perfectly legitimate one upon that hypothesis, or let its advocates shew the contrary) that the same absolute quality may be good at one time, bad at another; or that absolute qualities of opposite kinds may both be good or both be bad at the same time. If one being is formed to behold cruelty with the agreeable, kindness with the disagreeable emotion; if another being is formed in a way the reverse of this; when the one calls cruelty good, kindness bad; when the other calls kindness good, cruelty bad; the one pronounces something *absolutely true* of each sort of conduct as much as the other does. Cruelty is absolutely different from kindness, and kindness from cruelty, whatever emotions may be connected with the view of each.   But then *cruelty is as truly good in the one way as kindness is in the other.* This is the sort of consequence in which we maintain the absurdity lies, — a sort of consequence, in regard to which, I must repeat, that to tell us of the assertion of an absolute quality is nothing whatever to the purpose.

We shall look in vain to the writings of those who have supported the theory of a moral sense, for any effectual means of obviating the difficulties that attach to that theory.

All the account which Dr. Hutcheson can give of our ideas of the divine goodness, and of the rectitude of our moral faculty itself, is this.   The Deity possesses a principle of benevolence ; this principle necessarily led him to invest mankind with a sense to which actions promoting happiness should be agreeable.   Mankind, invested with such a sense, must necessarily view the divine character and acts in general, and, in particular, the act of bestowing such a sense upon them, with the agreeable feeling, i. e. reckon the divine character *good*, and the constitution of their moral sense *right*.

Now granting Dr. H.'s postulate of a benevolent principle in the Diety, as being matter of fact, — granting this fact to explain why we should have been formed to view beneficent actions with an agreeable emotion — granting (which I do not grant) that our consciousness alone had never actually distinguished any thing beyond a mere emotion in our moral determinations—granting all this, the real argument against Dr. H.'s system still remains in full force.

Where a question relates merely to this — what are the apprehensions of the human mind regarding any particular subject, such for instance as the nature of right and wrong,—we are not only at liberty, but really bound, to make every supposition regarding that subject that consists with mere possibility, if we would discover what suppositions are, and what are not, consistent with those apprehensions. He who would prohibit this, would prohibit the chemist from using, in his experiments, any substances or combinations of substances that are not found to exist in a natural state.

If we are capable of giving or receiving such an account of our own moral nature and ideas as that which Dr. H. furnishes, capable of stating, and of understanding, that we received our present moral sense in consequence of the Deity's possessing a principle of benevolence, and that his benevolence is good in our apprehenion solely in respect of our possessing such a sense,—if, I say, we are capable of stating and of understanding all this, we must be capable also of conceiving that the Deity might have had a principle of malevolence, and might have endowed us with a sense approving of malevolence. We must therefore believe that, if this had been the case, the Deity would have been as really, truly, and properly *good*,—a sense approving malevolence as *just* a sense as on the opposite supposition. — *Are* we capable of believing this ? *Is* this supposition consistent with our *actual apprehensions* of the nature of right and wrong ?*

If the supporters of Dr. H.'s system affirm this, I am unable to maintain the argument farther. If they are not in that case driven *ad absurdum*, I could never expect to bring them to it. If they cannot affirm it, then they must own that the receiving of an agreeable sensation from the view of an action, is not all that makes it right.

I feel entirely at a loss to discover, from an examination of the mode in which the theory I am considering has been supported, whether its defenders would choose to admit the conclusion just stated, or challenge the reasoning that leads to it. It appears to me that they go, so to speak, to the very verge of absurdity, and there stop; they will neither go forward nor backward; neither

* Undoubtedly Dr. H.'s explanation, in his own words, would be equally effective, if, to suit our supposition, we were to substitute *malevolence* for *benevolence.* Thus, " the present constitution of our moral sense determines us to approve all *malevolent* affections. This constitution the Deity must have foreseen as tending to the *misery* of his creatures. It does therefore evidence *malevolent* affection in the Deity. This therefore we must approve."

forward, to the effect of admitting explicitly that falsehood and cruelty would be truly and properly good, were any beings so constituted as to view these with the agreeable emotion; nor backwards, to the effect of having the error discovered, by which they have been led into a wrong track.

All this is granting Dr. H.'s postulate, that the Deity is possessed of a principle of benevolence. But it deserves consideration whether there are not, at the outset, obstacles to the admission of a system which makes this its very *starting point*, and which presents the divine benevolence in the light of mere experienced fact,* having no *visible* fixed connexion with the nature of intelligent mind. If a writer advances a particular theory of morals, and, instead of being able to assign, upon that theory, any reason why the Deity should have been disposed to perform an act of benevolence rather than the contrary, simply asks us to "grant such disposition" as the very basis of his argument, — if he gives no other explanation how any benevolent proceeding should have seemed *right* to the divine mind, than that the Deity had a *sense* approving of such proceeding, (that is, there was something in the divine nature which rendered such proceeding agreeable to the Deity,) and instead of shewing why such sense should have appertained to the divine mind, rather

* Besides that *as mere matter of fact* the proof of it is so far from being unexceptionable.

than one approving malevolent acts, gravely asks us to say "why it might not"*—surely it must be acknowledged that such a theory does not consist with our ordinary apprehensions of the necessary and unchangeable nature of the divine benevolence, or it ought fairly to be maintained that these apprehensions are absurd and groundless.

When, in order to evince the necessity of his supposition of the existence of a moral sense separate from reason, Dr. Hutcheson observes that "a being not possessed of a moral sense would see no propriety in one constitution's being given rather than another;" this is, or may be, just a truism and nothing more ; because a *moral sense* may denote generally the ability to perceive moral distinctions, in whatever that may consist ; in which use of the term, the proposition would simply amount to this, — a being who was incapable of distinguishing between right and wrong, could not discover any thing right in one constitution rather than another. To the same purpose it is to tell us that a being having no desire or wish to promote happiness, would not seek to promote it. The question is, could a rational being be *without* a moral sense, in this general meaning of a moral

* " Why may not the Deity have something of a superior kind, analogous to our moral sense, essential to him ?" The consequences of such a supposition as this, I shall afterwards have occasion to advert to. See page 85.

sense ?　Could a being be possessed of reason, and yet *not* see something right in the promotion of happiness, and wrong in the gratuitous infliction of misery?　It is plain that Dr. H., deceiving himself by the ambiguity of the expression " a moral sense," has here been led to beg the question.　He assumes that a being possessed of reason would, without a superadded sense, be incapable of discerning right from wrong ; and the affirmation which he has truly made of a being conceived to be destitute of moral notions altogether, should, in order to serve his argument, have been proved to hold good in the case of a being possessed of reason, but without a superadded moral sense.

On one occasion, however, Dr. H. discovers at once the necessity he has felt himself to lie under, of admitting the absolute nature of moral distinctions, and the utter contradiction which this notion receives from his theory.　And indeed it is to be remarked, that, while the supporters of this system have sometimes seriously endeavoured to repel the charge of its making moral distinctions to be merely relative, as if the establishment of this charge would be fatal to their system, they have, at other times, admitted the relative nature of such distinctions, in almost express terms. Nor does this remark apply only to different writers, but to the same writers in different parts of their works ; and its truth, I think, may be amply substantiated by a comparison of various passages quoted or referred to in this work.*

* It is somewhat surprising that Dr. Adam Smith should, in his examination of Dr. Hutcheson's theory, complain that that theory renders moral distinctions merely relative, without perceiving that the objections press with exactly the same force against his own theory.

" Yet surely," Dr. S. observes, " if we saw any man shouting with admiration and applause, at a barbarous and unmerited execution, which some insolent tyrant had ordered, we should not think we were guilty of any great absurdity in denominating this behaviour vicious, and morally evil in the highest degree, though it expressed nothing but depraved moral faculties, or an absurd approbation of this horrid action, as of what was noble, magnanimous, and great. So far from regarding such a construction of mind as being merely something strange, or inconvenient, and not in any respect vicious, or morally evil, we should rather consider it as the very last and most dreadful stage of moral depravity."

Now, what, according to Dr. S.'s theory, is wanting to make this man's conduct quite natural and approvable? Why, merely that he should be surrounded by an assembly of spectators, whose minds should be constituted in the same way with his own ; for then there would be that sympathetic agreement in their sentiments, which, according to Dr. S., gives birth to the sentiment of approbation — constitutes all that is meant by being right.

It is not less singular that Sir James Mackintosh (himself a supporter of the hypothesis of a moral sense) should make the same objection to Dr. Smith's theory, which Dr. Smith makes to Dr. Hutcheson's, while he apparently has not considered the objection as valid, or has not stated it to be such, against Dr. Hutcheson. So far as I can discover, the supporters of the sentimental theory have never been able to agree collectively,

In refuting the notion that our ideas of good and evil are derived from positive law, whether human or divine, Dr. H. observes, that " it must first be supposed that there is something in actions which is apprehended absolutely good, and this is benevolence, or a tendency to the public natural happiness of rational agents, and that our moral sense perceives the excellence." A few pages thereafter, we find the following: " If it be here inquired, Could not the Deity have given us a different or contrary determination of mind, viz. to approve actions upon another foundation than benevolence? It is certain there is nothing in this surpassing the natural power of the Deity."

Now can any one avoid perceiving, that, if there is an absolute standard of right and wrong, and if a moral sense can be constituted in two ways, an erroneous moral sense must be as conceivable, in regard to such absolute standard, as an unrighteous divine law; and, if there is absurdity in supposing that the divine law may be the standard of the rectitude of the divine law, is it not equally absurd to suppose that the determinations of a moral sense can be a standard of the truth of those determinations?

The way in which it evidently appears that Dr. Hutcheson and his followers have tried to reconcile, in their own minds, the absolute nature of the

or to resolve individually, whether they would admit or deny the absolute nature of moral distinctions.

divine goodness, (which they cannot get over,) with the doctrines of their peculiar theory, is by confounding together as one, the notion of the divine *benevolence*, and that of the *moral goodness* of that benevolence.   Benevolence is an absolute quality; and, this basis being established, an absolute standard is doubtless provided.   But the question necessarily occurs, how comes *benevolence* to be morally *excellent?*   Benevolence is morally excellent, we are told, because agreeable to our moral sense.   But our moral sense may be so formed, that benevolence, instead of appearing excellent, may appear vile and detestable.   In this case will our moral sense be wrong, or will benevolence cease to be excellent, or shall we make the one the standard for trying the other, that is, say that benevolence is morally excellent, because our moral sense determines it to be so, and our moral sense determines justly, because it determines benevolence to be morally excellent!   Is not this very satisfactory?   Let any argument employed * by the supporters of a moral sense, to

* Dr. T. Brown, in touching upon the point now considered, gives up, or at least does not contend for, the absolute nature of right and wrong; and thus, by going a step farther in maintaining absurdity, or a step less in admitting truth, avoids the inconsistency into which Dr. H. has fallen.   He shows that unless we had been previously constituted to approve of one kind of actions rather than another, obedience to the Deity would have appeared equally right when his commands

explain, upon their hypothesis, the absolute nature of virtue be examined, and this fallacy will be found lurking at the bottom of it.

Dr. Thomas Brown's vindication of the doctrine of a moral sense from the objections brought against it, rests entirely on the following points :

1st. " Right and wrong indeed signify nothing in the objects themselves." — " They are words expressive only of relation" (relation between an act and an emotion excited by that act) " and relations are not existing parts of objects or things to be added to objects or taken from them."— " But it is not to moral distinctions only that this objection, if it had any force, would be applicable. Equality, proportion, it might be said, in like manner, signify nothing in the objects themselves to which they are applied, more than vice or virtue."—" And if it be not necessary in the case of a science which we regard as the surest of all sciences, that the proportions of figures should be any thing inherent in the figures, why should it be required, before we put confidence in morality,

were of a malevolent, as when they were of a benevolent kind, which he justly takes for granted would not be the case *in respect of the way we are at present constituted ;* but this does not in the very least hinder the supposition, grounded on Dr. B.'s system, that our minds, though at present formed to approve of benevolence, antecedently to its being commanded by the Deity, might equally well have been formed to approve of malevolence.

that right and wrong should be something existing in the individual agents ?"

2nd. There is no reason for supposing that ever
our moral sense will be changed in its nature, so
as to make us view that as wrong, which we view
as right just now, and *vice versa.*

3rd. Even supposing reason to be the judge of
moral distinctions, reason itself may be overturned ;—and,—arguments founded on the possibility
of a change in our moral sense, are, no less than
those that question the rectitude of the reasoning
faculty itself, sceptical, and subversive of all inquiry.

In regard to the first point, it is almost superfluous to remark, that no one ever maintained the
absurdity that virtue or vice are, any more than
equality or proportion, " existing parts of objects
that might be added to objects or taken from
them." But has Dr. Brown meant to say, that,
according to his account of the nature of the
moral faculty, our moral determinations may be
of as fixed and unchangeable truth, as are the
doctrines of mathematics?—or, if he has not meant
this, wherein does he stop short of such an assertion, or what proposition, as distinct from this,
has he maintained? Either, I apprehend, he has
maintained this, or he has maintained nothing at
all. Let me ask then, when we perceive any of
the properties which flow from the nature of
mathematical figures, does our perception of such

properties depend upon something belonging to the figure, or upon something peculiar to the constitution of our mind, an alteration of which constitution would also alter the properties of the figure? For instance, is our perception of the equality of the angles of an equilateral triangle, one which an alteration of our constitution could convert into a perception, equally just, of their inequality? or, when we speak of mathematical truths, can it be said that we speak of what has "no universality beyond that of the minds in which the perception of these truths arises?" of "what our mind is formed" to perceive, "not of what it might have been formed" to perceive differently? Has the immutability of mathematical truth "regard only to the existing constitution of things, under that Divine Being who has formed our nature as it is?" Is it customary to ask no more foundation for the existence of mathematical relations, than that "they are relations which we and all mankind have felt since the creation of the very race of man," or to arrogate for them no greater degree of regularity than that of "the whole system of laws which carry on in unbroken harmony the motions of the universe?" or is it usual to represent the regularity with which mathematical truths hold good as being "sufficient for us while we exist on earth,"* and what

* Dr. T. Brown's Lect. 74, 75. See also Dr. Hutcheson's Illustrations, sect. 4.

we have no particular reason to fear will be interrupted afterwards ?

An entire perplexity of thought is visible in
that part of Dr. Brown's argument in which he
assimilates our perception of moral distinctions,
(as explained by his theory,) to our perception of
mathematical relations — a perplexity that arises
from his confounding the moral emotion, as one
act or state of the mind, with that other act or
state of the mind which consists in the perception
of a relation between that emotion and the action
by which it is excited, and then representing the
absolute truth of the relation thus perceived, as
an absolute moral character belonging to the action which moves the emotion. A relation between an action, and an emotion excited by that
action, may as truly exist as a fact, and be as
certainly perceived, as the relation between one
mathematical quantity and another. But would
not a similar relation exist, and be perceived with
the same certainty, under circumstances perfectly
the reverse — that is, where the same action that
now excites approbation should excite disapprobation ? If we could view the murder of a father by
his son with feelings of pleasure and approbation,
the relation between that act and those feelings
would remain equally real, and the perception of
it be as certain, as on the opposite supposition.

In regard to the second point of Dr. B.'s defence : —it is entirely idle to tell us of the *unlikeli-*

hood —(though how the unlikelihood exists I have never seen shewn) that cruelty will ever become morally good or kindness bad. What we ask is — *could* this be? Our question regards not probability, but possibility. *Could* cruelty, for its own sake, and because of its being cruelty, ever be good? If it could not, are we to suppose that an agreeable emotion cannot, in the nature of things, be connected with the view of cruelty, or that the particular emotion connected with the view of it is not what distinguishes it as good? These are the questions to be answered; but the questions — it somehow happens — that we never find answered.

What meaning, I would now ask, can we attach to the words, "We feel that it will be impossible, while the constitution of nature remains as it is, and we may say, while God himself exists, that the lover and intentional producer of misery, as misery, should ever be viewed with tender esteem," &c. Does the "constitution of nature" here mean that constitution by which we are formed to view an act productive of misery with the disagreeable emotion? If so, Dr. B. merely tells us that we can never view such an act with pleasure, so long as we remain constituted in such a way as to view it with pain. Does the "constitution of nature" mean the laws of thought or feeling, necessarily resulting from the nature of mind, as mind? If Dr. B. used the expression in this sense, he asserts the doctrine of his opponents, and contradicts his own. " We feel that it will be impossible" — by what faculty do we feel this? or rather,—as to *feel* a thing to be impossible is hardly correct language — by what faculty do we *judge* this to be impossible?—That faculty, whatever it is, is the ultimate source of moral notions.

Nor, in the last place, can it possibly avail Dr. Brown to argue, as he has done, that reason, as a faculty of our mind, has no more claim to remain unaltered, than the supposed capability of receiving the emotions distinctive of right and wrong; and therefore that the distinctions of morality will be no less precarious when ascribed to reason, than when traced to any other part of our constitution. Surely it must have been in an unthinking moment that Dr. B. composed this passage; or if the employment of an utterly untenable plea must attach a suspicion of unsoundness to the cause for which it is employed, never was there more ground for such a suspicion than here. What should we think, if any one were to maintain that the truth of this proposition,— " the whole is equal to all the parts,"—is not more necessary or universal than the truth of this other proposition,—" the touch of hot iron is painful." Yet such a point might be maintained by precisely the same argument that Dr. Brown has employed for the purpose of shewing that moral distinctions have no more stability when ascribed to reason, than to any other faculty. For suppose it were said, on the one side, that the constitution of our sensitive frame might easily be conceived to be so altered, that the touch of a hot iron might affect us in the most pleasurable manner, and that, consequently, the proposition affirming such touch to be painful, would then cease to be true, might it not be asserted, on the other side, that the faculty by which we perceived the truth of the mathematical axiom might likewise be perverted or overturned, since no principle of our nature had any "peculiar claim to remain unaltered in the supposed general alteration of our mental constitution?"* If this reasoning is good, so is Dr. Brown's reasoning good. They stand or fall together.

Into the question regarding the *rectitude of our faculties*, to which Dr. B. with more dexterity than soundness of argument, leads away the discussion, I am not in the least concerned to enter. There *are* certain truths which we are, at least, *under the necessity of conceiving to be absolutely immutable.* These truths we are said to discover by *reason.* We do not however infer their immutability from the assumed *rectitude* of reason; on the contrary, the *rectitude of reason* is only another way of expressing the clear and irresistible conviction we are *forced* to entertain of the certainty and immutability of these truths. To suppose then, that truths perceived by reason to be immutable, are yet not immutable; to suppose, in

* Dr. Brown's Lecture, 82.

other words, that reason may change, (for these two things are the same) *is to suppose a contradiction.* Is there the same contradiction in supposing that a disagreeable emotion might, at another time, be connected with the view of an action with which there is now connected an agreeable emotion ?

And now let me only ask what that doctrine must be *in itself*, of which *such* a defender can furnish but *such* a defence ?

SECT, III.

Inadequacy of the Supposition that Approbation and Disapprobation are mere EMOTIONS, *to explain the Phenomena of our moral Sentiments.*

In the preceding section, I have exhibited certain consequences of a most absurd kind, that seem inevitably to flow from that theory which makes moral distinctions to consist solely in the difference of the emotions with which we are formed to be affected, on the view of different actions. I have also examined the manner in which these consequences have been attempted to be obviated, which has appeared to me to be entirely unsatisfactory. I am now to endeavour to shew, independently of the absurd consequences which this doctrine involves, its entire *inadequacy*, of itself, to explain the nature of our moral sentiments, and the necessity which even its supporters have lain under, of adopting modes of speaking, utterly at variance with their own system, — modes of

speaking which must be understood as fairly proceeding upon the assumption, that certain ends or
actions are, in their own nature, fit and obligatory,
and that they are perceived to be so, by the faculty
employed in other cases in distinguishing truth
from falsehood, — that namely to which we give
the name of reason, the judgment, the understanding.

So long as our notion of *goodness* is that of one
simple quality belonging to persons or actions, and
by which alone, or by its opposite, they are morally distinguished — so long as an action is conceived to be something that can only be good or
bad, all other terms, such as obligatory, meritorious,
right, virtuous, being merely taken as synonymous
with good, or as, at most, expressing a difference
in regard to the point of time at which the action
is viewed — so long, it may be extremely possible
to explain, in a plausible manner, the moral goodness of an action, by representing it as consisting
merely in a certain emotion excited in the spectator. But if it is found, as I have endeavoured
elsewhere particularly to shew, that actions are
morally distinguished in many more ways than
merely as good and bad ; that various moral terms,
frequently taken as synonymous with good, are by
no means of convertible signification ; that an
action may have much of one moral quality in respect of which it would be denominated good,
very little of another in respect of which also it

would have been denominated good; that each of two actions, in short, may be better than the other, in different senses — if the moral qualities that may be ascribed to an action, are thus varied and complex, a theory calculated only to meet the supposition of a single distinguishing quality, cannot be expected to furnish any adequate solution of the phenomena it professes to explain.

Thus I can perhaps understand how it may be possible to apply to an action the qualities of good, right, proper, becoming, in the same way as we apply those of good, beautiful, pleasant, agreeable, to objects that excite certain bodily sensations, or certain emotions of taste; and to speak of such qualities, in each of the two cases respectively, as existing after the same mode.   But that *I ought* * *to do this* — that *I deserve to suffer punishment if I do that* — are propositions, my belief of which I am perfectly unable to identify with any species of sensation or emotion of which I can form an idea.

When we advert to the manner in which the na-

* " As to that confused word *ought*," says Dr. Hutcheson; " it is needless to apply to it again all that was said of obligation."   Sect. I.

It is no wonder Dr. Hutcheson wished to expunge the word *ought* from the language of Moral Philosophy.   It is the term most strictly and peculiarly expressive of a moral notion; the least admitting of being used in a loose sense; and therefore untranslateable into the language of any imperfect or erroneous system.

ture of moral *obligation* has been treated of, by the supporters of the theory I am considering, we shall discover, in the statements they have furnished, a very great degree of looseness and confusion.

Most, if not all, of those writers, have in a great measure lost sight of the distinction that subsists between acting from a sense of moral obligation, and acting from the impulse of any of the benevolent affections, some of which we have in common with the brutes. Thus they consider an agent as acting from a virtuous motive, who acts from the impulse of compassion, or even from that of parental, or filial affection. To say then that we are under a moral obligation, they just take to be synonymous with this, that such impulses and affections belong to our nature.* At other times they make the obligation to perform an action, to consist in this, that we shall find an advantage or gratification in it; and they are accordingly at pains to show, how some virtues, such as temper-

---

* " Having removed," says Dr. Hutcheson, " these falsely supposed springs of those actions which are counted virtuous, let us next establish the true one, viz. some determination of our nature to study the good of others; or some instinct, antecedent to all reason from interest, which influences us to the love of others : even as the moral sense determines us to approve the actions which flow from this love in ourselves or others." May we not gather from this, that a virtuous agent may exist without a moral sense at all? and that the inferior animals, in acting, as they often do, from benevolent instincts, must be viewed as acting *virtuously*?

ance, industry, frugality, benefit us directly; and how others, such as humanity, truth, justice, procure us the love and esteem of our fellow men, and are the means of obtaining us their confidence and their good offices in turn.*

* Mr. Hume, after explaining the nature of obligation in this manner, is forced to make the admission after all, that there are some cases in which it is not for our interest to be virtuous. The way in which he passes over the difficulty in which this admission involves him, is well worth marking.

" Treating vice with the greatest candour, and making it all possible concessions, we must acknowledge that there is not, in any instance, the smallest pretext for giving it the preference above virtue with a view to self-interest, except perhaps in the case of justice; where a man, taking things in a certain light, may often seem to be a loser by his integrity. And though it is allowed that, without a regard to property, no society could subsist, yet, according to the imperfect way in which human affairs are conducted, a sensible knave, in particular incidents, may think that an act of iniquity or infidelity will make a considerable addition to his fortune, without causing any considerable breach in the social union and confederacy. That honesty is the best policy, may be a good general rule, but is liable to many exceptions. And he, it may perhaps be thought, conducts himself with most wisdom who observes the general rule, and takes advantage of all the exceptions."

The philosopher proceeds : —

" I must confess that if a man think that this reasoning much requires an answer, it will be a little difficult to find any, which will to him appear satisfactory and convincing. If his heart rebel not against such pernicious maxims, if he feel no reluctance to the thoughts of villany or baseness, he has in-

Now in regard to these statements I would merely observe, that, if the moral goodness of an action consists, as we are told, solely in this, that it excites a pleasant emotion in the beholder, then to speak of any action as being obligatory, either in respect that we are prompted by certain affec-

deed lost a considerable motive to virtue; and we may expect that his practice will be answerable to his speculation. But in all ingenuous natures, the antipathy to treachery and roguery is too strong to be counterbalanced by any views of profit, or pecuniary advantage. Inward peace of mind, consciousness of integrity, a satisfactory review of our conduct, these are circumstances very requisite to happiness, and will be cherished and cultivated by every honest man, who feels the importance of them."

Does not Mr. Hume here virtually admit, that, according to his principles, it is impossible to establish, in all cases, a moral obligation to observe the laws of justice? " If his heart rebel not against such pernicious maxims, if he feels no reluctance to the thoughts of villany or baseness." — Well; what ensues on this supposition? " He has lost," we are told, " a considerable motive to virtue."

Nay; but I should say that, upon this supposition, he is not, on Mr. H.'s principles, at all under an *obligation* to practise justice. If the man feels no reluctance to injustice, if he has no interest in refraining from it, we have *exhausted*, as regards his case, all the grounds of obligation that Mr. Hume allows us. If we still say that the man is under an obligation, we at most only say so with as much truth, as we might tell that a certain kind of food or drink is exquisitely pleasant and wholesome, — to a person who should feel his stomach turned by it. It might be pleasant and wholesome to us; certainly not to him.

tions of our nature to perform it, or that we have an interest in performing it, is to make an action to be *obligatory*, in a way totally unconnected with that in which it is *morally good or right*.   Indeed obligation, as explained in either of these ways, would be felt to exist independently of that faculty, which is yet represented as the only source of all moral notions.   For undoubtedly we have impulses prompting us to certain actions, and could perceive that a certain mode of conduct would be advantageous to us, even if we had no moral faculty at all.

To say however that man possesses, in the constitution of his nature, an impulse or propensity to perform certain actions ; or that a certain line of conduct is most for his true interest or advantage : neither of these expressions is identical or the same with this, it is his *duty* to perform such actions, or to follow such line of conduct.   On the other hand, if the latter proposition is said to be an inference from one or both of the former ones, if it is a man's duty to act so and so, *because* he is impelled by a propensity in his nature, or *because* it is his interest, we are still left to inquire, what is *meant* by duty or obligation ; or by what faculty the perception of duty or obligation takes place. And if the notion of obligation is a *moral* notion, if it is derived from the moral faculty, the supporters of the theory under consideration are bound to explain the nature of obligation, on the principle on which they explain the nature of moral distinctions in general. If they cannot do so, their principle is incorrect or deficient. It is not enough to establish the existence of extrinsic motives to virtue. They must show how an obligation to practise virtue arises out of its very nature, as they explain its nature. But this can only be done by supposing the obligation to perform an action to mean, simply, that a certain pleasant emotion will be felt by the agent, if he perform the action, a painful emotion if he omit the performance. This, accordingly, is the view given by the more consistent and exact defenders of the doctrine.*

Now, in the first place, a reference might be made to every man's consciousness, and to the structure of ordinary language, whether there is not a perceivable distinction between performing an action under the notion that it is *right* or *our duty*, and performing it for the sake of the pleasure we find in reflecting on the performance; whether the pleasing reflection is not felt to presuppose the duty instead of making it.† But, taking the case as supposed, it is obvious that

---

* See Dr. Brown's definition quoted in page 79. The additional circumstance of the *feeling excited in others* by the view of the agent's conduct, can affect my argument but as matter of degree, that is, — in the nature of that argument — not at all.

† So far as my reasoning is concerned, to enjoy the pleasing, to avoid the painful emotion, may be taken as the same thing.

if, when a man is strongly bent upon some object of advantage or pleasure, all that is meant by saying that he *ought not* to gratify his desire, is, that a painful feeling will ensue upon the gratification, it becomes—if this is the whole case (and we are assured it is the whole case)—a simple matter of calculation which of the two courses will be, in the gross, the most pleasant, or the least painful,—a matter in regard to which an agent might and would undoubtedly put the question to himself, whether or not he *ought* to incur the painful feeling rather than forego the desired gratification.   Now that surely cannot be a correct account of the manner of our distinguishing right from wrong, according to which account we might rationally ask whether or not we ought to do what we distinguish as wrong ; and even, in some cases, (for all that appears at first view,) rationally answer in the affirmative.

The error then of those who make moral distinctions depend on the determination of a certain sense or taste, appears to be of precisely the same kind with that of those who make them depend on civil laws, or the will of the Deity.   To the two opinions last stated it is justly objected, that they leave a question behind them, — why is it obligatory to obey civil laws or the will of the Deity.   Does not the other opinion leave a similar question—why is it obligatory to please the moral sense or taste ?

The works of the supporters of the doctrine of a moral sense, abound with sentiments such as these — that "nature has designed it to be the guide of life," that it is "plainly the judge of the whole of life,"—"the governing power of man;" "that it naturally assumes a right of judging;" that "we must deem it necessary to enter upon that course which it recommends;"* that it "was given us for the direction of our conduct;" that it "carries the most evident badges of this authority;" that "it is set up within us to be the supreme arbiter of all our actions." So also—"Every sense is supreme over its own objects. There is no appeal from the eye with regard to the beauty of colours, nor from the ear with regard to the harmony of sounds, nor from the taste with regard to the agreeableness of flavours. It belongs to our moral faculties, in the same manner, to determine when the ear ought to be gratified, when and how far every other principle of our nature ought either to be indulged or restrained."†—Now such sentiments as these, vary them how we will, can only bear one of two meanings — either that we always *do* act so as to obtain the agreeable emotion, or that we always *ought* to act so. That we do not in fact always act so, is but too well known. That we ought to act so, is a proposition, the mere *truth* of which (even supposing that

* Hutcheson.   † Smith.

F 2

could be satisfactorily proved) does not, it is obvious, tend one jot towards a removal of the difficulty that has been stated.   It might be shewn that *we ought* to obey the laws of God, the laws of the land; would this remedy the unsoundness of the two theories founded respectively on these principles ?

But besides, the proposition — *we ought* to do what excites the agreeable emotion, — translated into the language of the theory under consideration, must mean, simply, that it *excites the agreeable emotion,* — ("*we ought*" signifying nothing more) — to do what excites the agreeable emotion, — so that we find ourselves again just exactly where we were, at the question, namely, — why we ought to do what excites the agreeable emotion.

If we more closely examine the manner in which the advocates of a moral sense generally express themselves, as if in regard to this difficulty, we shall find that they balance undecidedly between the two following positions—indeed they have no other alternatives to choose between. Sometimes they seem to speak as if the proposition, — we receive an agreeable emotion from the view of some actions, a disagreeable emotion from the view of others, — were, to all intents and purposes, *identical* with this — we ought to prefer the gratification arising from this emotion to any other gratification.   But to assert this, is just to assert any thing whatever that one pleases to assert. Of a mere emotion of pleasure which, whatever its *specific*, absolute or relative, nature, is still *but an emotion of pleasure*, and one which is not always *in fact* preferred to every other gratification, it can never be an absurd question to ask whether or not or why *it ought* to be preferred. That we ought to act so as to obtain the agreeable emotion (supposing the existence of the capacity alluded to,) may be a true proposition, or a false proposition: I may grant that it would be a true one; but it would not be an identical proposition.

But, in the next place, the advocates of a moral sense sometimes speak as if the two propositions—an emotion of pleasure attends the performance of certain actions—we ought to seek this pleasure above all other pleasures—were not identical, but the latter a deduction from the former, the former a reason for the latter; or they connect the two propositions, thus standing as premise and inference, by various intermediate processes: thus, — that we ought to act so as to obtain the agreeable emotion *because* it constitutes our highest felicity, *because* it appears to be the intention of nature, the intention of our Creator; *because* our being made susceptible of such emotion indicates the probability of a future state of rewards and punishments,—and the like. Now, for my part, supposing that we have such a capacity as described, I should be inclined to say these were just reasons why we ought to do such actions as we are constituted to behold with an agreeable emotion; but then it is abundantly clear, that to shew a *reason*, however just and cogent, *why* we ought, does not explain the nature of this perception itself—*we ought*. Nay the entertaining of the question at all, why we ought to do those actions which we contemplate with an agreeable emotion, the assigning of reasons of any kind for our doing so, affords the most direct proof imaginable, that what *we ought* to do, and what *occasions an agreeable emotion*, cannot possibly mean one thing.

I have already observed, that, if the supporters of this doctrine, in urging that we ought to do what excites the agreeable emotion, use the expression "*we ought*" in the meaning which their own theory assigns to it, their proposition, so explained, is quite a nugatory one for their purpose, as still leaving us to ask the very question which that proposition is meant to answer or exclude. If they do not use it according to their theory, what becomes of that theory? Can any thing be more evident than that they do *not* so use it, and that they really, in this case, make the emotion not the *source*, but the *subject* of a moral determination? The necessity, then, which they feel themselves under, of urging the proposition in question (in all the various shapes which I have instanced) exhibits the fatal defect of their theory, namely,—that the authority of the supposed moral sense is not of an original or final kind, or such as to exclude a previous determination as to its right of supremacy. On a just theory of morals it could never be necessary to establish, as a principle, that we ought to do what is agreeable to the moral faculty. This would be an identical proposition, admitting neither of question as to its own truth, nor of any further inquiry beyond it.

But it will perhaps be argued, that such expressions as these — we ought to obey the dictates of conscience — we ought to do our duty — are in frequent use, and may be presumed to consist with a true theory, whatever it may be; and, consequently, that if the use of these expressions, or others of similar import, attaches any difficulty to the theory of a *moral sense*, it must be a difficulty from which no system whatever can be free.

In reply, I would observe in the first place, that we employ the expression *"we ought"* on two different occasions. At one time, we speak in regard to a man's ignorance or disbelief of something that he ought to do; at another, to his disinclination to do it. Here, supposing his inclination, we speak of what he ought to do, in opposition to something contrary or different which he ought not to do; there, supposing his knowledge, of something which he ought to do, in opposition to his neglecting or being averse to perform it. In the one case, the expression is intended to supply ignorance or correct error; in the other, to stimulate inactivity or combat aversion.   When we say, a man ought to perform any *specified* duty, the expression may be significant, whether as used to inform or to impel. He may be ignorant that it is his duty; he may be indisposed to perform it, even while acknowledging it to be his duty.   But when we say that a man ought to perform his duty, or to do what is agreeable to conscience or the moral faculty, *generally*, the proposition can only be significant when used to impel; used to inform, it must be entirely tautological; since what is agreeable to conscience, and what he ought to do, plainly mean just one thing.   We suppose, in this case, certain descriptions of actions to be already distinguished as what ought to be done, in opposition to others different which ought not to be done; and our proposition necessarily has reference not to an agent's doubt or ignorance, but to his disinclination or neglect.—It will not, I think, be denied that this is the way in which these expressions are, in fact, used; and that any theory according to which we cannot use them to the effect that we do in fact, or necessarily use them to a different effect, cannot be a just theory.

Now if the proposition — we ought to perform certain descriptions of actions — imports something that is perceived by reason to be *true*, it cannot, as a truth, be more or less than a truth; and it may, as what cannot, at least, be denied to be truth, be properly and fairly urged in regard to an agent's insensibility to, or neglect of it. The case is wholly altered when we suppose the proposition in question merely to mean that the performance of a certain description of actions is attended with a pleasant, or the omission with a painful, *emotion.* To urge this upon an agent, is to urge upon him a point which he can best determine for himself; and if he knows that his moral feelings are weak or blunted, or that he can suppress the painful feeling (and who will deny that the mere *feeling* of conscience may to a certain extent be thus suppressed?) he may, in a comparative sense at least, deny the obligation to exist in his case; for this he does by simply saying — the agreeable emotion I scarcely feel: the painful one, I can deaden or dissipate by new gratifications. On this theory, then, the proposition used in regard to an agent's disinclination, may be, in a great measure, nugatory.

But still, if the proposition in question were, upon the theory of a moral sense, *merely* used in an emphatic or persuasive way, there would be no occasion at present for remark. The grand objection to that theory is, not that — supposing the proposition to be used thus,— it could not be used effectively; but that it is *not used thus;* that it is, and must be, used as a significant proposition, not to *impel,* but to *inform.* That we ought to do what is agreeable to the moral faculty, is, on that theory, at least a disputable point; it is what we require to be informed of, and even to have reasons assigned for believing.

And although, upon a just theory of morals, it can never be any thing but an absurd question, to ask, as a matter of truth or falsehood, whether or not we ought to do our duty, to follow the dictates of conscience, or of the moral faculty, (which yet, I contend, upon the hypothesis of a *sense*, is a real and fair matter of question in this respect,) yet as such a question may always be asked in regard to an agent's inclination or disinclination — as an agent who acknowledges something to be his duty, may still, in consultation with himself or others, put the question, shall I do my duty or not? — it becomes possible for us, besides urging, emphatically, that he *ought* to do his duty, to offer supplemental or cumulative grounds why he ought to do so.   Thus, we may tell him of the satisfaction he will enjoy in the testimony of his own conscience, and in the applause of other beings,— of the rewards annexed to virtue in this world, and of the apparent intentions, or the expressed commands, promises, and threatenings of the Deity. But these, I repeat, are merely additional or auxiliary grounds.   They are intended to operate on the mind chiefly as sanctions, motives, inducements, persuasives; not by any means constituting the reason why one ought to do his duty — for such reason is essentially implied in its being his duty — but determining his choice, and strengthening his resolution to do it; not affording conviction that was wanting, but impulse that may be superadded. At the same time every consideration such as described, really creates a new duty. For instance, if my everlasting happiness depends upon my performing certain actions, obligatory in their own nature, the performance of such actions straightway becomes obligatory for that of itself, that such is the consequence of performing them, and independently of the original obligation; because obligation would arise in such a case, even in regard to an action originally indifferent. Still, this consideration cannot be necessary to shew that *I ought to do my duty*, as regards the original action, if that action, really, and in its own nature, was my duty.

After what has been said, it is almost unnecessary to observe, that so far are the opposers of the doctrine of a *moral sense* from questioning the *supremacy* of the moral faculty, that their reasoning necessarily assumes this supremacy. The moral faculty (such as their argument) is supreme; on the hypothesis that this faculty is merely an *emotion*, its supremacy cannot be explained — therefore, the hypothesis is a wrong one.

It is by no means an uncommon fallacy in reasoning, in those cases where the explanation and the thing to be explained are capable of being easily substituted for one another, to represent the truth of the former as established by arguments which only serve to establish the truth of the latter. The fallacy may be plainly exhibited in cases where this substitution is more difficult. Were a person to assert that the good crop of last season was owing to the bad seed time, it would be very natural for us to maintain, that a bad seed time, instead of producing a good crop, would certainly tend to produce a bad one. Now, what should we think if told in reply : — You are quite mistaken in your argument, for there can be no doubt whatever that the crop has been an excellent one ! Extraordinary as this logic may appear, it is really no other than what has been employed in defence of the doctrine of a moral sense. We object to that doctrine, that, if our perception of duty is resolvable into a mere desire or feeling, no reason appears, why that desire or feeling should be gratified more than any other affection of our nature. How do they reply to this? simply by asserting (as they are well entitled to do *) that the moral sense ought, without doubt, to be gratified, in preference to any other principle of action. They treat the argument of their adversaries as denying this position ; and in successfully maintaining it, in asserting the supremacy of the moral sense, they prove the truth — not certainly of their explanation, but only of the thing to be explained.

* That is, in the general signification of the expression *moral sense*, as denoting the *moral faculty whatever may be its nature*.

No one who gives sufficient attention to the foregoing considerations, can now, I think, feel any difficulty in perceiving how the matter really stands, namely, that the advocates of a moral sense, while representing that sense as the sole percipient of right, duty, obligation, what ought to be done, are nevertheless obliged to assume, in a manner inexplicable upon their own supposition, and really *in the exercise of their reason*, that the moral sense *ought* to be the supreme guide of our conduct. In other words, their theory cannot maintain itself without the assistance of that other theory which it is meant to displace.*

On the whole, the effect of the argument we have been offering will appear to stand thus:

If we define or describe the moral faculty in

* The notion of virtue's being merely a sort of taste, seems not entirely removed from a certain species of practical judgment that may occasionally be met with. We shall sometimes see a man incur the same sort of disapprobation and dislike, because he would not serve a friend or benefactor at the expense of his duty, as if his attachment to duty had been something like an attachment to poetry or music, — the indulgence of which, though innocent in itself, and even laudable, incurred the charge of selfishness, if allowed to oppose the claims of friendship or gratitude. It is worth observing, that even such a notion as this supposes an ultimate perception of duty not identical with a mere taste, since it could only be expressed in words to this purpose — that a man *ought not* to indulge his taste for virtue when the calls of friendship or gratitude require its being denied.

any other way, than merely as the faculty by which we perceive that we *ought* to do some things, avoid others,—that is, if we define or describe it in any way, in which the affirmation, that we *ought to gratify the moral sense*, will be any thing more than an identical proposition, we inevitably lay ourselves open to this question,—why ought we to obey the moral faculty? This must always, in such a case, be a question of real meaning, and a question to which no satisfactory answer can be given.

On the other hand, if we are compelled to define the moral faculty, as I hold that we are, simply as the faculty by which we perceive that we ought to do some things, and to avoid others, it is clear that we can give no other account of our perception of moral distinctions, but that we perceive it to be *true* that we ought to do some things, avoid others. If all that we can say of this proposition, is, that it is a true proposition, this is equivalent to saying that *reason* perceives it to be true; for we have no other idea of reason. So, conversely, to ask if we ought to do what reason decides we ought to do, would be to ask if we ought to do what it is true we ought to do, i. e., if we ought to do what we ought to do.

It is evident that the same sort of consequences that, in the preceding section, were shown to attach to the hypothesis of a moral sense, in regard to the moral character of an agent or an action as existing or past, will apply to the obligation previously lying on an agent to perform or avoid any action. The obligation to perform or avoid, will exist, not absolutely, but as relative to his constitution; so that he must conceive that, were he differently formed, he would be as truly and properly under an obligation to exercise every species of injustice, deceit, and cruelty, as he is, at present, to avoid these acts. Would it be possible for a man who should have this apprehension of the nature of moral obligation, to feel any regard for it?

The likeness found by Dr. Brown between our sense of moral obligation and our belief in the uniformity of the laws of nature, entirely fails in regard to the very important particular now adverted to. " It is all which we mean by moral obligation," Dr. B. tells us, " when we think of the agent as feeling, previously to his action, that if he were not to perform the action, he would have to look on himself with disgust, and with the certainty that others would look on him with abhorrence." Now is it all that *we* mean by the uniformity of the laws of nature, that we have a *trust* in this uniformity?" Would an alteration in our constitution, by which we should cease to expect the sun to rise, or a stone that is thrown up to fall, prevent the sun from rising, or the stone from falling, or make it true that these events would not happen?

Even then, if it were granted to Dr. B. that our belief in the constancy of the laws of nature cannot be traced to any thing essential to the nature of mind*, that belief is (unlike our belief, as Dr. B. would explain it, of the existence of obligation,) a belief of something not relatively, but absolutely true.

Similar considerations to what have now been offered in regard to the notion of obligation, and to the entire inadequacy of the theory under review, to explain that notion, apply also in regard to the notion of *moral desert* of reward or punishment. In like manner as the supporters of that theory have, in a great measure, confounded the obligation to perform an action, with the desire we feel to perform, or the advantage we derive from performing it, so they have generally, to a similar extent, confounded our perception of good or ill desert, with the mere animal impulses of gratitude and resentment ; or ascribed our sense of the fitness of rewards and punishments, to a view of the benefits thence resulting to society. Now it is obvious that so far as we explain an agent's desert of reward or punishment, to mean simply the gratitude or resentment we feel towards him, our explanation of desert proceeds without the supposition of a moral faculty at all, and therefore fails of presenting it as a *moral* notion.   The dog that bites us, or the bee

* See *Appendix* to this section.

that stings us, may be said, upon such an explanation, to perceive our desert of punishment. So, if the benefit resulting to society is what constitutes the desert, a soldier killed in battle *deserves* to die. But, if the notion of desert is conceived not in regard to others, but to the agent himself, and if it is strictly a moral notion, it must be traced to the moral faculty; and, in consistency with the theory I am considering, to say that an agent deserves reward or punishment, ought to mean precisely this, and nothing else, viz.: either that the emotion of approbation or disapprobation carries along with it a desire to benefit or hurt the agent approved or disapproved; or that the contemplation of such an agent enjoying reward, or suffering punishment, affects us with an agreeable emotion.

It is needless to repeat, in regard to this representation, objections of an entirely similar effect to what have been already offered. Nothing would appear to be more clear than this, that, when we say, a man ought to be rewarded or punished, we assert something of him, not of ourselves; that his desert, in either way, is quite independent of any thing desired or felt by us; and that we feel bound, in innumerable instances, to regulate the gratification of our love or resentment, — to sacrifice the satisfaction we should feel in beholding a person affected with good or evil, to our idea of his *desert*, as something totally different from any mere feeling or affection we can entertain in regard to him. No mere *feeling* with which *we* can be affected, can possibly mean the same thing with this, that *he deserves* reward or punishment; or preclude us from asking the question, why he ought to receive good or evil, merely because we desire it, or should be pleased at it : — a question, which, if we do not answer, we leave a difficulty unsolved : if we do answer it, it is by reasoning in a circle : but which we cannot even profess to answer, without acknowledging it to have a fair intelligible meaning ; and acknowledging consequently that the desert of an agent cannot mean the same thing with any affection or emotion felt by us.

From what was advanced in the preceding section, it might naturally be expected, that the patrons of the system I have been opposing would be particularly apt to betray an inconsistency, whenever they should come to speak of the character of the Deity, either in general, or as displayed in the endowing of certain orders of beings with faculties distinctive of right and wrong. It is obvious that if, on such occasions, the writers in question pronounce of the character or acts of the Deity, that they are *good*, or apply to them any terms whatever expressive of moral qualities, they pronounce such judgment, or apply such terms, in the use or exercise of their own *moral faculty*, whatever it may be. And if their expressions, as then made use of, are entirely undistinguishable from the determinations of reason, as declared on other occasions,—clear and intelligible when taken as the dictates of reason, and yet utterly nugatory and unmeaning, because necessarily involving an argument in a circle, when considered only as denoting that certain sensations or emotions have been felt by those who utter such expressions, — surely the insufficiency of the hypothesis maintained by these authors must become glaringly apparent.

"I shall not," says Dr. T. Brown, "attempt to picture to you the *wretchedness*— the wretchedness of a world in which such feelings were not a part of the mental constitution;"—and again, "But if, in the minds of different individuals, this distinction were differently formed, it is evident that the social happiness and even the social union of mankind could not be preserved. It is necessary for general peace, that there should be some great rule of conduct." — Now suppose any person to ask here, — *why should not* the state of man be a state of *wretchedness,*— of wretchedness, beyond description? why should the social happiness, the general peace, *be* preserved? Had any person put such questions as these to Dr. B. would he not (and justly) have judged the querist insane? and must not his expressions be taken as those of a man, who, in the ordinary exercise of his *reason,* assumes the truth of such propositions as these— "Man *ought not* to be wretched," — "It is *right* that the social happiness, the general peace should be preserved, rather than the contrary?"

But suppose, for a moment, that Dr. Brown does not here speak in the use of the faculty which generally discriminates truth from falsehood, but in the use of that faculty, another and different one, that discriminates right from wrong — just as he might discourse upon the natural beauty of external objects, in the exercise of the power of taste. He determines then that men received the capacity of distinguishing right and wrong, for the sake of their happiness—because they would have been wretched without such capacity. Put the question then again,—why not? Because their being wretched would be viewed with the emotion of disapprobation. And why should they possess the capability of this emotion? because they would be wretched without it—and so on. Is not this very satisfactory reasoning? Let Dr. B.'s expressions then be otherwise translated into the language of his theory.

" We can discover nothing in the nature of our minds," Dr. Brown elsewhere observes, " which should enable us to perceive a distinction between right and wrong; but we may discover why our mind has been so constituted. It has been so constituted by the goodness of God for the sake of our happiness." — Now there are just three meanings that can be affixed to this, and the supporters of the views I am considering will have to choose among them.

By saying that we find the reason of our present moral constitution "in the provident goodness of God," Dr. B. may mean simply that we received this constitution because the Deity, *in fact*, desired to make us happy. —Now this, let it be observed, is just the same sort of explanation that it would be to say, that plagues and earthquakes have happened because the Deity, in fact, desires us to be miserable. In the one case, as in the other, we just infer the intention from the effect—then conversely again the effect from the intention. — If this is a satisfactory explanation, surely philosophers have taken a great deal of unnecessary pains in accounting for the origin of evil.

But again; by saying that we owe our moral constitution to the provident goodness of God, Dr. B. may mean that God gave us this constitution because it was *morally right* to give us such a constitution. But morally right, in *our* apprehension, means, according to Dr. B.—"affecting us with the agreeable emotion"— in this sense his proposition will amount to this—we received this constitution, because its being given is agreeable to this constitution.

But suppose Dr. B. to mean by *morally right*, morally right in the *divine* apprehension, i. e.

agreeable to a capacity of emotion in the Deity similar to ours. — If the promotion of happiness, as an end or effect, is, *in its nature,** an object calculated to excite this emotion in the divine mind, — that such is its nature, must surely be something that the *divine* reason at least is capable of apprehending. The moral fitness of this effect then cannot depend on the mere fact of the emotion, but on the nature of the effect being such (i. e. on there being something of such a kind *true* concerning it) that it must excite this emotion. To grant this would be granting all that, for my own part, I feel much anxiety in contending for. To grant that something is thus *true,* in the nature of things, of the promotion of happiness, as an object or end, something which reason, in its nature (whatever particular degrees of it may be) is capable of discovering to be true, — is to give up all that is material in the controversy. To deny this power to human reason would then be, to say the least, an entirely arbitrary determination. But indeed if moral good and evil be different things as regards the divine mind, from what they are as regards the human mind, there is an end of all speculation on this subject, and on every matter connected with natural and revealed religion. The *divine goodness* would be a phrase without meaning.

* If not, the case must, in some way, resolve into the *first* explanation.

Many other passages of a similar import to those now examined, might be produced from Dr. Brown's work. In like manner, Dr. Adam Smith, with his wonted elegance and justness of thought, exhibits, in a variety of instances, the utility, the final causes, of different parts of our moral constitution ; and expatiates on the goodness of God, in forming that constitution as it is. We find, then, that those who place the essence of right and wrong in the *feeling* of the spectator, yet suppose that the capability of such feeling was not arbitrarily implanted in us, but implanted, by the goodness of our Creator, for the sake of our happiness, as a *final cause.* Now it seems to me that our very notion of a final cause, is that of a reason why any thing *ought* to be ordered as it is: a fit, or right purpose, end, or aim, to be answered, in its being so ordered. Unless the notion of a final cause involves that of an absolute and independent moral fitness, to show that a contrivance produces pain, would be assigning just as good a final cause for it, as that it produces pleasure; nor can we adequately describe or explain a final cause, but by terms expressive of moral notions, and consequently implying a moral faculty. In pretending then to assign a final cause for the existence of a moral sense, we assign a final cause for that part of our nature, without which we could not yet form the very notion of a final cause. — When the authors I have been al-

luding to, thus assign a final cause, can any one
doubt that, in the very act, they *make a moral determination*, or doubt that this act is an act of
their reason ?

I before stated grounds for hazarding the assertion that the supporters of the theory I am opposing, really speak in the exercise of their *reason*,
when they say that *we ought to be guided* by the
supposed moral sense. On similar grounds I have
now felt warranted in representing them as speaking in the exercise of their reason, when they
determine that it was *right we should receive* such
a sense, as being conducive to our happiness. To
those who may think me justified in these repre-
sentations, I need not point out the absurdity of
supposing that reason can perceive it to be *right*
that we should have such a sense, *right* that we
should follow it, and yet that reason, without
such sense, cannot at all determine between right
and wrong.

Even then on the unnecessary, (as it appears to
me,) though certainly not impossible supposition,
that such a capacity of emotion, as that which has
been specially denominated the moral sense, exists, I feel entitled to contend that it is not the
determinations of this sense that make virtue or
vice; that it may be a direction, and incentive to virtue ; virtue, however, otherwise conceived of : so
that actions would be essentially virtuous or vicious,
even if there were no such sense, or a sense con-

stituted on a different principle : and in short, that the implanting of such a sense by the Creator, presupposes that he perceived an intrinsic excellence in what the sense was given to lead us to ; without which no such sense would, to the best of our knowledge, have ever been given.

Certainly the existence of such a sense is an object about which our reason or understanding can be employed, as well as about the existence of our memory or imagination ; and whether it was *right* that we should possess it, whether we *ought* to be guided by that sense or not, are questions which, do what we will, we cannot remove from the cognizance of reason ; so that if a moral sense really existed, it could not yet be the ultimate judge of right and wrong, in so far as it may itself be an object about which such judgment is employed.

APPENDIX TO SECT. III.

Of the Nature of our Dependence on the Constancy of the Laws of Nature.

It appears to me that our belief in the constancy and uniformity of the laws of nature, is resolvable into our perception, *that every effect (change) must have a cause:* which implies, that we suppose every thing to remain the same as it once is, or has been, until there is a cause for change or alteration. The continuance then is the rule, the change, the exception ; and we do not inquire why a thing should have remained as it was, but why it should not have remained, if it has undergone any alteration. If I find a stone lying on the ground where I left it yesterday, I do not ask, how has it happened to remain there? but, if it has been removed, I ask, — how has it been removed? In like manner, if the stone continues of the same figure or colour, I do not imagine that this requires to be accounted for; but should its figure or colour have changed, this does require to be accounted for. All this seems very plain in respect to the figure or appearance of the stone; but suppose that any *power* has been once found to belong to it, such as that of exercising a particular chemical action on certain other substances, and we straightway ask, as something requiring to be explained, why we should expect this power to operate again, because we have seen it operate once? Just for the same reason, I should answer, that we expect to find the stone lying on the table where we had left it five minutes ago, and whence nobody has had an opportunity of removing it. The power here supposed to belong to the stone, is as much conceived to be permanent (bating the operation of other causes) as its size, figure, or position; and whatever reason exists for expecting it to continue unchanged in any one of these particulars, creates the same expectation in regard to any other.

It is evident, however, that this explanation

presupposes the notion of a *power* belonging, as a quality, to material substances; and this very notion of a power, has been represented by Dr. Brown as itself depending upon that law of our nature, by which we calculate upon like events succeeding like causes. But I apprehend our notion of power does not at all depend upon our experience of several sequences, but arises inevitably upon the perception of a single change. Although the experience of several sequences may be necessary to enable us to connect particular effects with particular causes, the notion of *cause* in general, arises on the perception of a single effect or change. Now the very notion of a cause involves that of *power : cause* is, in its very meaning, *power :* and, as I have said, a power once perceived to belong to any substance, must be expected to continue in it, until cause appears for the contrary.

There is, in the case under consideration, a sort of double application of the principle referred to; one of a positive, and one of a negative kind. The process may be thus exemplified. When, for the first time, I apply my hand to the conductor of an electrical jar, the shock I experience immediately suggests the notion of a *cause*, by which such effect has been produced — i. e. of something that has *power* to produce the effect. This is the positive application of the principle. Without farther experience, however, it is very likely I may not be able to pronounce that the contact of my hand with the conductor, is *the* cause. Two or more trials, however, make me believe that this contact is the *particular cause* of the extraordinary sensation I have felt; in other words, that the conductor has a *power*, on being touched, to produce this sensation. On this ensues the negative application of the principle. To suppose that every change must have a cause, is to suppose that no change takes place without a cause. So long, then, as there is not actual reason for supposing a cause for change, so long there is no positive expectation of change; so long we expect every thing to continue the same. And a power once imagined to belong to any animated or inanimate being, is undoubtedly what enters as intimately into our general conception of that being, as any other component part of that conception; and we as little expect any change or cessation of that power, when no cause of such change is, on positive grounds, apprehended to take place, as we expect a change or cessation of any thing else which makes the being to be what it is. In short, I expect the power of the electrical jar to continue, for the same reason that I expect the figure of the jar to continue, or the jar itself to remain where I left it.

And on careful consideration it will appear, that we cannot so properly be said to expect the continuance of the laws of nature, as not to apprehend the discontinuance of these laws. Accordingly, whenever a law appears to be interrupted, we do not satisfy ourselves with saying, why should we have supposed that this law would always continue? but we straightway look for an actual cause for its discontinuance; and according to the degree in which we can suppose such causes to intervene, our dependence on the constancy of a law is lessened.

We conceive of a *power* as resident either in a material substance, or in a living mind (whether the former can be conceived, but as caused by the latter, is not the question here)—and where we refer the power displayed in any of the operations of nature to the volitions of an agent, the supposition that he acts by design, * or, at least, that he does not change his mode of acting without reason, preserves our expectation of uniformity the same as in the case first supposed.

Thus, the continuance of the sun's rising and setting, is either conceived by us as resulting from a power residing in that body, and of which a change is no more to be looked for, than in his size or figure, or as resulting from the power of an in-

---

* A writer in Blackwood's Magazine endeavours to explain the matter entirely on our perception of design. I do not think this a sufficient explanation. But the thought seems, so far, a just one; and I do not remember to have met with it elsewhere. — **Remarks on Natural and Revealed Religion,** vol. i.

telligent agent, who will continue to have the same reasons for this exercise of his power as formerly; or at least will not discontinue the exercise of it, but for a reason. The material inquiry then is, not why we should suppose the sun to continue his revolution, but why we should suppose he would not. And accordingly, our belief is not so properly the positive one, that the sun will rise, as the negative one that nothing will occur to prevent his rising; and at all events our belief is not as of a certainty, but of a high probability.

SECT. IV.

Of positive Arguments against the Supposition that REASON *judges of Moral Distinctions.*

Looking to the difficulties which press upon the opinion that moral distinctions exist merely as the consequence of a peculiar susceptibility of sensation or emotion belonging to the spectator,—looking also to the insufficiency of this opinion in itself to explain the phenomena of our moral sentiments,—it might be supposed that the theory opposed to it, that, namely, which represents such distinctions as the subject of certain truths resulting from the nature of things, and perceived by reason, the judgment, or understanding, must be liable to some objections of extraordinary magnitude, if its pretensions, as has generally been the case, have been passed over in a slight and superficial manner by those who reject it. Yet on the most diligent search for such objections, I can say, with truth, I have been able to find literally none, which do not resolve either into a mere assertion of the matter in dispute, or into the maintenance of some point not at all inconsistent with the conclusions to which it is sought to be placed in contradiction. What may pass for such objections, will be found reducible to one or other of the three following heads.

I. One class of arguments seeks to prove, on positive grounds, the existence of a moral *sense* as a distinct faculty: the effect of which, if established, might be, to make the use of reason, as a moral faculty, appear either inadequate or superfluous.

But the arguments that are employed for this purpose, prove, not the existence of such a faculty as opposed to reason, but as opposed to an entire insensibility to moral distinctions; or as opposed to self-love, considered as the sole spring of human actions. Of this let the following passage from Dr. Hutcheson serve as an example.

"That this sense is implanted by nature is evident from this, that, in all ages and nations, certain tempers and actions are universally approved and their contraries condemned, even by such as have in view no interest of their own. Many artful accounts of all this, as flowing from views of interest, have been given by ingenious men; but whosoever will examine these accounts, will find that they rather afford arguments to the contrary, and lead us at last to an immediate natural principle prior to all such views."

No one could here be at a loss to perceive, that the *moral sense* just means, in general, the power of distinguishing right and wrong, in whatever that power may consist. The ambiguity of the term *moral sense* is not always so visible; else Dr. H.'s hypothesis had not maintained itself so well.

II. A second class of arguments proves, not that moral distinctions cannot be perceived by *reason*, but that, in order to perceive them, we do not, in every case, employ *reasoning* — meaning, deduction of conclusions from premises by several successive steps. To this I readily assent, since most moral truths are perceived intuitively. Like mathematical axioms, however, they may be perceived by *reason*, though without *reasoning*.

III. But the objection supposed to bear with the greatest force against the doctrine which makes reason the ultimate judge of moral distinctions, is founded on the great difference which is conceived to appear between approving or disapproving of an action, on the one hand ; and judging between truth and falsehood, on the other.—In the effects which are produced on our minds by the view of a generous, a tender, a heroic deed, do we find, it is asked, nothing different from what is experienced in giving our assent to one of Euclid's demonstrations ? Is our mind similarly affected on beholding an act of treachery, and in discovering a flaw in an argument? Surely, it is argued, effects so different can never result from the operation of one and the same principle.

That the mind is similarly affected on beholding an action, and contemplating a proposition, no body, I suppose, will maintain : nor is it a fair statement of the matter in dispute to make this the subject of question.   An action and a proposition are essentially different; and no comparison can be instituted between them.   The point in dispute is not whether an emotion is not felt at *beholding* an *action;* but whether reason cannot judge of certain *propositions* regarding that action *whether it is beheld or not.*   The comparison then is properly to be made between a moral proposition and any other sort of abstract proposition—as, for instance, a mathematical one : and the question is, cannot reason judge of the truth or falsehood of the one, as well as of the other? Now so far as appears to me, I can decide upon the truth or falsehood of such propositions as these, "happiness ought to be promoted rather than misery,"—"a promise ought to be kept," — "it is fit that virtue should be rewarded rather than vice," — with as little emotion or mental excitation, as I can determine that four times nine is the same as twice eighteen.

It will, with the utmost readiness, be rejoined to this, that I may make such affirmations regarding actions, in the same way as I can affirm that sugar is sweet, without experiencing at the time the sensation of sweetness ; but that, in like manner as it is only by having formerly experienced the taste of sugar, that I can now attribute to it this quality, so it is by having formerly experienced the emotion of approbation or disapprobation at beholding certain actions, that I can now attach to these actions the qualities of right and fit, or the contrary.   But is this any thing more than an assertion of the point in dispute ? Is there any argument ? any proof ? — Distinguish, I pray, between the proof and the thing proved.

That emotions of the most vivid kind are experienced, when certain species of actions are actually performed, or even fancied to be performed, before us, is most true, and cannot but be true. But does the mere fact that these emotions are thus excited, by the real or fancied *performance* of the action, prove, either that we cannot, in the exercise of our reason, affirm any thing of such action, without beholding, or fancying the performance of it, or that we cannot affirm it to be right or wrong otherwise than in reference to the fact of the emotion? or even in the case of an action, really performed before our eyes, can the emotions that are then felt exclude the possibility of a previous, or present judgment of the understanding, that such action ought or ought not to have been performed ? Because emotions are felt, does it follow that no judgment has taken place, or can take place? Because I am pleased at seeing a benevolent action, indignant at a cruel or perfidious one, is it therefore impossible for my reason to determine, that the one is right, the other wrong? or even when I do not behold the action, can I not perceive this without a reference to any actual emotion, experienced or anticipated, simply on the case being proposed to my understanding? What you have to prove is, that there is *not* a judgment — all that you prove is, that there *is* an emotion.

It seems to me then, that those who have denied to reason the power of discerning moral truths, have always stood aloof from the points which their adversaries maintain; and have applied themselves exclusively to the establishing of certain other points, true in themselves, but by no means explaining all the phenomena of our moral determinations, nor in the least impugning those views of a different cast, which have been urged by other theorists. They tell us, the contemplation of particular actions excites in us certain agreeable or disagreeable feelings; — this is true : — that those which excite the former, we call good, those which excite the latter, bad;—true also. They tell us, farther, that every act of an agent supposes some affection, desire, or feeling, as the motive of that act ; and that there is no identity or even similarity between a feeling or emotion, and a judgment of the understanding. Even let all this be granted likewise. But then, on the other hand, here we produce certain *propositions,* declaring some things to be right, others wrong ; and we call on you to say, are not those propositions *true*, and is it not *impossible they could ever be false* ? If you own this, you own them to be necessary truths ; if you own them to be necessary truths, you own them to be discerned by reason : you own, then, so far, that reason can judge of moral distinctions. Let this point rest on its own merits ; and if, besides this, there are emotions raised on the view of such actions, when *actually beheld ;* or if a desire intervenes between the exercise of the reasoning faculty and the *performance* of the action,—we must explain these as we best can. But where does there appear to be any clashing between the one thing and the other ? between the judgment and the feeling ? To what purpose then the perpetual cry, we have an emotion, and an emotion is not an act of reason?

I repeat then, that simply to allow the *necessary truth* of one moral proposition, is sufficient to put to rest all question as to the instrumentality of reason in our moral determinations. Reason can at least do something in these determinations. Whatever is perceived to be necessarily true, must be from something in the nature of that concerning which it is perceived, and not from any peculiarity in the constitution of the percipient being ; and nothing can be discovered to be necessarily true, but by the power of reason.

A favourite remark with all those writers who have denied to reason the power of distinguishing between right and wrong,—one on which they always appear to lay particular stress,—is this: Reason, say they, may indeed be usefully employed in discovering the means by which that which is agreeable to any faculty may be obtained; but reason can never discover what is thus agreeable. This argument, which contains at once an affirmation and a denial, is of service to those who make use of it in two ways. Their apparent readiness to own what is to be owned, lends some degree of authority to what they deny; while the semblance of pointing out a way in which their adversaries may have been misled, is apt to pass for a proof that these have actually been so misled. But is it not obvious that, in what they deny, they just beg the question? Do they not here simply assume, that right and wrong are merely things that are agreeable or disagreeable, merely objects of desire or aversion to the beholder—the very notion which it is the aim of their opponents to controvert?

" Fitness, as understood by every one, is obviously a word expressive only of relation. The fitness of virtue for producing serene delight, is not, as mere fitness, greater than that of vice, for producing disquietude and wretchedness; and we act therefore as much according to the mere fitness of things, in being vicious, as in being virtuous." Brown, Lect. 76.

It is fit that a man in distress should be relieved:

—Fit, in relation to what? only to the satisfaction which we experience in seeing him relieved? Is the thing then not fit in itself? Is it possible that any one can say, there is no reason for relieving misery, but the pleasure we take in seeing it relieved? that there is an equal fitness in causing misery, provided only that we took a pleasure in it? Is not reason at least as cognizant of the fitness of the end, as of the fitness of the means to produce that end?

Dr. Adam Smith, after defining, in the manner now alluded to, the extent to which reason can be employed in determining what is right and wrong, has the following observation: "As reason, however, in a certain sense, may justly be considered as the principle of approbation and disapprobation, these sentiments were, through inattention, long regarded as originally flowing from the operations of this faculty. Dr. Hutcheson had the merit of being the first who distinguished, with any degree of precision, in what respect all moral distinctions may be said to arise from reason, and in what respect they are founded upon immediate sense and feeling. In his 'Illustrations upon the Moral Sense,' he has explained this so fully, and, in my opinion, so unanswerably, that if any controversy is still kept up about this subject, I can impute it to nothing but either to inattention to what that gentleman has written, or to a superstitious attachment to certain forms of expression," &c.

I have examined the treatise here referred to, with all the attention that is due to the high talents of its author, and to the powerful authority by which it is, in the present instance, recommended: nor does it at all appear surprising to me, that Dr. Smith should have considered the reasonings it contains as unanswerable. Unanswerable I believe they are, in regard to the points which they are directed to maintain ; —but those points, I apprehend, *are not the points at issue.*

Dr. Hutcheson proves, or justly asserts, that in so far as virtue is an exciting cause or motive to *action,* there must be something that is an end to the agent, or immediately desired by him ; and that in so far as an agent justifies or approves of an action after it is performed, he must have some sensation or emotion of satisfaction, pleasure, or complacency in it. He likewise proves unanswerably, that any reason that can be given as a motive to action, or even for the preference of one end to another, still implies, (I will not allow, *presupposes*) some ultimate end desired for itself ; and justly holds that the *desire* of an end, is not an act of reason.

Now there is not a single point here maintained, that the advocates of reason would deny. They allow, that virtue cannot possibly be a principle of *action,* but as it implies some desire to perform the virtuous act ; some satisfaction in, or after, the performance of that act. But they assert that this desire, this feeling of satisfaction, is the *consequence* of perceiving something to be right, not that in which its being right consists. Dr. H. on the contrary assumes, that its being right *means no more* than that the agent has this desire or satisfaction; that this desire or satisfaction is the *original fact beyond which we cannot go:*—but, I ask, do any of his reasonings prove this? does he attempt to prove it?

It is surely neither an irrational nor unphilosophical inquiry, to ask, how any desire springs up in the mind; what precedes or occasions it: nor does it at all preclude such an inquiry to tell us, that any reason that can be assigned as the exciting cause of an action, must bring us to some desire in the end; that there can be no exciting reasons previously to *affection;* that ends cannot be intended without desire. These are truisms; and without disputing (which would be utterly absurd) that an end necessarily implies some *desire,* may we not still ask—not, for what more remote end do we desire the present end (for this would produce questions *ad infinitum*) but, — how does the desire of the ultimate end itself arise?— A person desires that some one would ring the bell: why? because he desires to speak with the servant. Why desire this? because he desires that dinner should be brought. Why, again? because he is hungry. And what means hunger? — All that we mean by hunger, Dr. H. would

say, is, that a man desires to eat, or would feel a
a gratification in eating : and here too, according
to him, we should be at the end of the inquiry,
and could go no farther.   But would it be very
absurd to ask again, why one desires to eat?—not
as asking *for what ulterior end* he desires to eat,
(which would undoubtedly be absurd) but, merely,
how does the desire come to exist, how is it to be
accounted for, in what condition or circumstance
of the bodily organs does it spring up ? or would it
be very absurd to answer, that it arises from an
empty state of the stomach, and that to the sensation thence arising, we give the name of Hunger?
Hear, then, as applied to this instance, the argument against the instrumentality of reason.   Before
a man eats or calls for food, we must suppose that
he feels some desire to eat, or that he will experience
some gratification in eating ; it is impossible that
eating could be an *end*, that there could be any
motive to the action without this—*therefore* hunger
cannot be owing to any thing in the state of the
stomach ; for an empty stomach and a desire are
two perfectly different things.—Is not this sufficiently preposterous ?

If a desire, then, may ensue upon a particular
state of a bodily organ, why may it not ensue upon
a particular perception of the intellect ? Indeed,
what is but a conjunction of fact and experience
in the one case, is one of necessity in the other.

And if, in stating the intellectual perception, we

only pretended to advance a step farther into the inquiry, the aim would be strictly legitimate. But it is not, in the present case, merely a step in advance beyond another, previously found sufficient to explain the phenomena; for it has been elsewhere shown that the previous step, without this additional one, is entirely insufficient for that purpose : since, instead of presenting us with a principle to which we may trace the phenomena to be explained, it only describes one class of those phenomena themselves. It is as if one who proposed to explain philosophically what is death, should say, it is an inability to exercise the bodily or mental faculties.

If, then, it can be shown, as has been elsewhere attempted, that the mere fact of our desiring to perform certain actions, or that of our receiving an agreeable emotion from the performance of them, does not give an adequate account of the nature of right and wrong; and if a previous inquiry into the nature of that fact itself is both rational and possible, then by this prior inquiry may we expect to discover wherein right and wrong consist. And an account every way adequate is accordingly to be found in the supposition, that the faculty of reason perceives certain actions to be right, others wrong; a supposition too, which will be found of itself sufficient to explain why we desire to perform certain actions, and feel a delight in the performance of them, either by ourselves or others.

But the objection now considered, as well as some others which cannot be so well introduced at this stage, will be yet more completely removed, when we come to take a fuller view of the origin and nature of our moral sentiments.

Thus I have endeavoured to exhibit the entire similarity that subsists between our moral judgments, and those other judgments, which are universally ascribed to the principle of reason. I have displayed the absurd consequences that follow from supposing our perceptions of right and wrong to be mere sensations or feelings, resulting from our peculiar constitution ; and have tried to show the entire failure of all the efforts that have been made to obviate those consequences. I have next attempted to evince the inadequacy of the doctrine that involves these consequences, to explain, even independently of such, the phenomena sought to be explained ; and have finally adverted to the remarkable want of positive arguments in support of that doctrine, or in opposition to that in support of which I have been engaged. I have now only to add the indisputable fact, that the common forms of language are entirely in favour of the supposition, that *reason* is the judge of *right* and *wrong*.

The whole question, indeed, as regards its essential merits, and the points on which its determination hangs, seems to me to stand simply thus :

There are two different descriptions of propositions, each of which may be, respectively, true or false, but in different ways: an example of the one kind is to be found in those propositions which state the sensible qualities, or the beauty and deformity of outward objects; of the other, in mathematical truths. The difference between these two species of truths consists in this, that the last flows from our very conception of the object contemplated; the first does not: the contrary of the last contradicts possibility; the contrary of the first contradicts at most but fact. That all the parts are equal to the whole, results from the very nature and meaning of half and whole. That a rose has a pleasant smell, that a Grecian temple is beautiful, does not result from our conception of these objects, (provided that the pleasant smell in the one case, the visible beauty in the other, are not made component parts of the conception,) and we can easily conceive them to want these qualities, or to have different ones. To say that a Grecian temple is not beautiful, or that a rose has an unpleasant smell, may be untrue; but to say that all the parts may be less than the whole, is not merely untrue, but absurdity and nonsense.

The matter in dispute is,—do moral propositions, or at least *certain moral propositions instanced,* more resemble the first, or the last of these species of truths?

Take the proposition that an agent ought to promote his own happiness and that of others rather than their misery.—Does this truth, or does it not, flow from the conception of the objects to which it relates? Does the contrary (or even the negative) of the proposition contradict fact only, or also possibility? Is it *possible* that it could ever be *right* for a being to seek his own misery and that of others?

If one man were so constituted as to find the smell of a rose pleasant, another so constituted as to find it unpleasant, (which is surely possible,) it would be just as true that the perfume of the rose was bad as that it was good; as true that it was good as that it was bad.

If one man were constituted to behold the intentional production of misery by a living agent with an agreeable emotion, another with a disagreeable emotion, (which also is surely possible,) would it be as true that the production of misery is right, as that it is wrong? This is matter of a simple appeal to the mind.

If this appeal is answered in the negative, it then appears that there is at least one moral proposition, the truth of which flows from the nature of the objects considered, and the contrary of which can never be true. This proposition then possesses all the characters of the last species of truth described, and such characters as do not belong to the first. – I know nothing more that could be required to show that such moral proposition is an absolute necessary truth perceived by reason, and that reason is, so far — and as much farther as other propositions of similar character can be found—a judge of moral distinctions. There is no other criterion that I know of by which the point could be determined.

I am fully aware that the whole hinge on which my arguments turn, is this, — that there is some thing, be it what it will, *immutable* in moral truth. This I am forced to assume—prove it I cannot. Grant this,—no matter how sparingly, how nakedly, or how much in the abstract; no matter how fettered with suppositions or provisions,—and all that I contend for will follow. Deny this, and the whole argument will indeed fall to the ground.

APPENDIX TO CHAP. III.

THE first rough draught of this treatise was composed, before the publication of Sir James Mackintosh's learned and interesting "Preliminary Dissertation" in the new edition of the Encyclopedia Britannica,—or at least before I had an opportunity of perusing it. My confidence in some of the opinions advanced by me has been infinitely strengthened, by observing their coincidence with those of so competent a judge. And I think it will be found that, in particular, the views expressed by Sir James as to the prejudice which the philosophy of morals has sustained from the confounding together of two different branches of the inquiry, and those which he has offered regarding the relation of *utility* to virtue, will, in the course of the present work, meet with some useful illustration and extension.

On one point, however, the system of Sir James is directly at variance with that which I have felt myself constrained to adopt. The doctrine which represents *reason* as the primary source of moral distinctions, he has treated less as being of questionable or doubtful truth, than as an exposed and almost abandoned error. Indeed the establishment—for as such he views it—of the contrary doctrine, that which I have been at so much pains in endeavouring to controvert, he generally marks as one of the most signal and obvious advances that the theory of morals has effected in modern times.

Considering the weight that is due to the opinions of Sir James Mackintosh on this subject, and also the nature of the composition in which these opinions have been put forth, (a composition which, as being professedly a general historical view of the science, appears to stand in the same relation to an ordinary controversial writing that the summing up of the judge does to the pleading of the advocate, and to be entitled to as much more trust,) I may be pardoned for briefly applying the general views offered in the preceding chapter to the specific points urged by Sir James, so far at least as these do not appear to have been already directly met.

No proof is furnished by Sir James, or any of the sentimentalists, that an emotive act attends every exercise of the moral faculty. In all their arguments on this point, the sentimentalists confound these two things—perceiving an action to be right, and, desiring or willing to perform a right action. Their constant argument is, * before an action

---

* Thus, " What could induce such a being to *will and to act ?" —" Reason, as reason, can never be a *motive to ac-

can be *performed*, there must be a desire or act of will on the part of the agent. Granting this, is it not possible to *perceive* an action to be right and yet *not perform* it? or cannot an action be made an object of thought, without performance, without the possibility of performance? But if an action may be perceived to be right, without the agent's yet performing it, this perception of its being right may exist anterior to any emotive process: for it is only upon the supposition that the will is moved, that the sentimentalists can ground the necessity of a desire or emotion; and they cannot shew that the will is moved, when the action is not performed.

tion;"—" when the conclusion of a process of reasoning presents to his mind an object of desire, a motive of *action* begins to operate, and reason may then, but not till then, have a powerful though indirect influence *on conduct*," (Prel. Diss.) —so the whole paragraph,—" Let any argument to *dissuade a man from immorality*," &c. " It is then apparent that the influence of reason on *the will* is indirect"—" through whatever length of reasoning the mind may proceed in its advances towards *action;*"—" some emotion or sentiment which must be touched, before the springs of *will and action* can be set in motion."—To the same purpose Dr. Thomas Brown: " If we had not previously been capable of loving the good of others, as good, and of hating the production of evil as evil; to shew us that the happiness of every created being depended on our choice, would have excited in us as little eagerness *to do*," &c. Brown, Lecture 76.

How happy would it be, if, as these writers have seemed to understand, the *perceiving* of what is right, and the *doing* of it, did not mean different things!

But besides, if an action cannot be right, but as an agent wills or desires to do it, it follows, that it must be more or less right, according as he has more or less desire or will to perform it ; and that if he has no will or desire to perform it, it is not right at all. To quiet the conscience, to remove obligation, would thus be one and the same thing : to say that a man did not desire or will to do an action, would be to say that he was not under a moral obligation to do it. In the following passage, Sir James Mackintosh so fairly lays open this weakness of his system, that I am astonished how he was not led by the absurdity of the consequence, to discover the error in his premises.

"Let any argument to dissuade a man from immorality be employed, and the issue of it will always appear to be an appeal to a feeling. You prove that drunkenness will probably ruin health. No position founded on experience is more certain. Most persons with whom you reason, must be as much convinced of it as you are. But your hope of success depends on the drunkard's fear of ill health : and he may always silence your argument, by telling you that he loves wine, more than he dreads sickness. You speak in vain of the infamy of an act to one who disregards the opinion of others ; or of its imprudence, to a man of little feeling for his own future condition. You may truly, but vainly, tell of the pleasures of friendship, to one who has little affection. If you display the delights of liberality to a miser, he may always shut your mouth by answering, ' the spendthrift may prefer such pleasures : I love money more.' If you even appeal to a man's conscience, he may answer you, that you have clearly proved the immorality of the act, and that he himself knew it before, but that now, when you had renewed and freshened his conviction, he was obliged to own that his love of virtue, even aided by the fear of dishonour, remorse, and punishment, was not so powerful as the desire which hurried him into vice."

Here a case is put, where a man is supposed to acknowledge that the immorality of an act has been proved ; while at the same time he declares himself desirous and willing to commit this immorality ; or at least, that any desire he has to avoid it, is overcome by a stronger desire.—If the immorality of the act has been proved, while yet the *will* is not moved, then surely the immorality cannot depend upon the will's being moved, or upon the existence of any emotive process : nay it must depend upon something else.

If a man were to say, My conscience prompts me to pursue a particular mode of conduct, but stronger desires prompt me to the opposite mode of conduct ; it would indeed be in vain to argue farther with him—meaning by the expression *in vain*, that we should have no means of bringing him to action. But even after a man has told us that his conscience is overpowered by stronger impulses or desires, or that he does not regard his conscience; and after we are satisfied that he will not act according to conscience; could we not still, with perfect truth, and with intelligible meaning, say to him,—Whether you are inclined to act so or not, — whether you regard the dictates of conscience or not, this is still *your duty* —what you *ought* to do; and it is neither more nor less your duty, upon account that you will or will not do it: and if we could justly say this, is it not abundantly clear that an emotive process is not the principal element, nor even any element at all, in the perception of right; but merely an attendant upon that perception, which may attend it in a greater or less degree, or, comparatively speaking, not at all ?*

I must confess I am unable to see where the difficulty lies, in answering the challenge contained in the following words.

" No advocate of the intellectual origin of the moral faculty has yet stated a case, in which a mere operation of reason or judgment, unattend-

---

* Perhaps it might be said here, that a desire's being overcome by a stronger desire, is not the same as if such desire did not exist at all ; and therefore that the rightness of the action might still consist solely in this, that there was a desire to perform it, — that an agreeable emotion would have been felt in performing it — though some opposing inclination might, in effect, prevail. According to this explanation, if we told a man that something was his *duty*, whether he desired or willed to perform it or not, we should merely be telling him,— whether you are disposed to do this or not, you would be disposed, if you were not more disposed to do something else !

ed by emotion, could, consistently with the universal opinion of mankind, as it is exhibited by the structure of language, be said to have the nature or to produce the effects of conscience. Such an example would be equivalent to an *experimentum crucis,* on the side of that celebrated theory. The failure to produce it, after long challenge, is at least a presumption against it, nearly approaching to that sort of decisively discriminative experiment."

First. If, by desiring to be shewn a case, in which a mere operation of reason or judgment, unattended by emotion, could be said to have the nature, or to produce the effects of conscience, Sir James means a case, in which reason, of itself, and previously to any emotion, can determine that an action is right or wrong; to talk of producing such a case, is much the same as to talk of producing a case of a man's being able to move his arm or his leg. It is wrong to inflict pain on an innocent man; wrong to deprive him of all his property; right to save his life if he is likely to lose it; right to restore him what has been taken from him. Surely I can determine that these are true propositions, without any emotion whatever. Oh! but say the sentimentalists, you would have an *emotion* before or after you performed these actions, or upon seeing them performed; and all that you mean just now, by saying they are right or wrong, is, that *you feel you would experience these emotions.*— Is not this just asserting the point in dispute?

Secondly. If Sir James desires to be shewn a case, in which an act of pure intellect, a mere intellectual perception of truth or falsehood, can have *all* the effects attributed to *conscience*, in the ordinary, and the just, signification of the term; that is, in which an act of intellect will, in itself, be desire, and emotion, and volition; —he asks a case to be produced, in which that which is nothing but an intellectual perception, will be something more than an intellectual perception ; in which a thing will be more than it is, or what it is not; which is absurd;—but who, I may ask, has ever maintained such an absurdity ?

But thirdly. If he asks the production of a case in which the act of intellect *gives birth* to the emotive process ; in which a man first perceives by his reason that something is right, and where that perception is inevitably followed by a, desire to perform such action, perhaps by the actual performance of it ; and where an emotion of satisfaction as inevitably follows such performance: if, in other words, he asks the production of a case where the supposition of the intellectual perception will account for the emotion : then I apprehend such case is produced, wherever an instance of virtuous conduct is produced : and I am at a loss to understand how the existence of the desire, volition, or emotion, can in this case disprove the existence of the previous intellectual perception, — not to say how it can be accounted for without it. — Suppose a man were to maintain, that we mean nothing more by saying, — it is day, — than simply this, that we can exercise the sense of sight, by discovering and distinguishing the objects about us; and suppose any one were to deny the identity of these two propositions, and to assert, that, by saying — it is day, — we meant that the sun had risen, and was giving light, — what should we think of his being met with a demand like this, — shew me a case where the rising of the sun, without our seeing and distinguishing objects, could be said to have the nature and effects of day! — The term *day*, here, has just the same sort of vagueness and comprehensiveness, as the term *conscience*. As the one includes the absolute and independent fact of the sun's rising, and the constant attendant of that fact, namely, the sensations of sight in us, so the word *conscience* includes the judgment that something is right, and the emotion we feel in regard to the performance of it. Even then if it were owned (which it is not) that the emotion does not more necessarily and invariably attend the judgment, than our perception of visible objects does the rising of the sun, would this be to own that the judgment does not take place, or that it may not be an independent fact — of which the emotion is, in certain cases, the attendant — as much as the rising of the sun is an independent fact, though invariably followed with our perception of visible objects? And is there, to say the least, any thing more inexplicable in this, that the emotion, the desire, should ensue upon the view of an action, apprehended by reason as *right*, than that it should ensue upon the view of one simply apprehended as *beneficial?* Even granting the intermediate mental process (namely the perception, that what is beneficial is right) to be unnecessary for an explanation of the emotion, can it be said that it obstructs such explanation? Even granting that the emotion *inexplicably* follows the mental perception that an action is right, does it less inexplicably follow, — even on the scheme of the sentimentalists, — the perception that it is beneficial? But the intellectualists do not even allow that the emotion is inexplicable. They argue thus: The action is beneficial; it must necessarily appear right: if it appears right, the performance of it must necessarily cause an agreeable emotion. The sentimentalists say — the action is beneficial; the view of it, we know not why, does, in fact, excite an agreeable emotion. — Which of these, I ask, has most reason to tax the other with failing to explain the emotion?

I have already adverted to a method, by which the sentimentalists attempt to obviate the fundamental objection to their theory. The following remark of Sir James Mackintosh, is an exemplification of its use. " That the exclusion of reason reduces virtue to be a relative quality, is another instance of the confusion of the two questions in moral theory; for though a fitness to excite approbation, may be only a relation of objects to our susceptibility; yet the proposition, that all virtuous actions are beneficial, is a proposition as absolute as any other within the range of our understanding."

But if virtue is (as Sir James's theory makes it) only "a fitness to excite approbation;" and if to be " a relation to our susceptibility" is to be only "a relative quality," it must, I think exceed ordinary penetration to discover how virtue can, after all, be other than a relative quality. All that we can here learn to be absolutely true of the action is that it is *beneficial*. But *beneficial* does not express a moral distinction at all, more than *difficult* or *easy* does; it is but the subject of a moral distinction. We could discover an action to be beneficial (i. e. productive of happiness or pleasure) even if we had not a moral faculty. Our question is, in what way do we perceive a *beneficial* action to be *right*. What is meant by moral distinctions being absolute, is, that the *rightness* is absolute; so that any one who— whatever were his peculiar constitution— should say that a beneficial action was wrong, would be affirming what was, and always must be, false.

I am unable to see that the objection, the validity of which is now insisted upon, confounds, as Sir James asserts, the two great questions which he distinguishes. On the contrary, I must be pardoned for thinking that the ingenious author himself, in this instance, confounds both these questions with a third which is different from either. It is one question to ask, what is the common quality of those actions which we denominate right; and to this it is, or may be, a just answer, to say, that this quality is their beneficial tendency. It is another question to ask, by what faculty of our minds we perceive actions to be right. To this one party answers that there is, in our constitution, a susceptibility of receiving an agreeable emotion from the contemplation of those actions, and a disposition to perform them: another party, that our reason, on the conception of a beneficial action, perceives of such action, that it is right. But there is still a third question, which has arisen out of this difference of opinion, and it is quite distinct from either of the other two; this, namely, — what is *meant* by an action's being *right?* That this is different from the first question, would be owned even by those who suppose that the beneficial tendency of an action is what makes it right. That a beneficial action is right, is not a definition, but a proposition. *Right* and *beneficial* are not the same thing. But the sentimental theorists would make one answer serve both the second and third questions. That an action is right, means, according to them, nothing else but that we receive an agreeable emotion from the view of it. The intellectual theorists again, being asked what they mean by *right*, at once answer that they cannot tell. The notion is familiar and clear to them, but they hold it incapable of definition; and the very thing they

object to the opposite party is, that these furnish
a definition of it — at least, that they describe it
as consisting in an *emotion*, if they do not pretend to distinguish the nature of the emotion.
They assign the *genus* of right, if they cannot assign its *species*. The intellectual theorists neither offer to tell its species nor genus. Now, supposing the sentimental theory to be true, the
quality *for which* an action is right may indeed be
an absolute quality, but not the quality of right
itself. If *right* be an absolute quality, the sentimental theory cannot explain it as such.

Like most of the theorists of his peculiar school,
Sir James struggles hard to make it appear, (yet
only by mere dint of assertion,) that it is implied
in the very existence and nature of the supposed
moral sense, that we ought to do what is agreeable to it, rather than what any other bent of our
nature prompts us to do, — overlooking that the
very pains he takes to inculcate the preference
due to this sense, shews that its right to such preference is, at least, liable to question ; and that,
if this can be made even a question, *without obvious absurdity*, then it cannot be implied in the
existence of such a sense, that we ought to prefer
its gratification to any other gratification. " Passion," says Sir James, " implies nothing but an inclination to follow it, and in that respect passions
differ only in force." And what does the moral
sense imply, but that the gratification of some
particular passion may be attended with a certain

feeling of pain? Will any one say, if the case stands simply thus, that it is not at least a rational question to ask whether I *ought* to gratify my passion, with this pain, or escape the pain and disappoint my passion? " No notion can be formed of the principle of reflection or conscience which does not comprehend judgment, direction, superintendency; authority over all other principles of action is a constituent part of the idea of conscience." No notion can be formed of *conscience*, which does not comprehend judgment, direction, or superintendency; but a notion can be very easily formed of a mere *desire* or *emotion*, which does not comprehend these. And here lies the fallacy of the sentimental argument.* Its supporters argue well the supremacy of conscience — but not the supremacy of such a principle as they describe conscience to be. It is extremely hard to see how " no notion can be formed" of a *mere emotion or desire*, " which does not comprehend judgment, direction, superintendency;"

* The only way of depriving them of the benefit of this fallacy, is to avoid the use of the word *conscience*, or even *moral sense*, altogether in the discussion — though this necessarily occasions circumlocution. The question is not regarding conscience, — the moral sense; but regarding a *capacity of agreeable and disagreeable emotions*, pretended to be that in which conscience or the moral sense consists. That the conscience, the moral sense, ought to be supreme, is allowed on all hands. The question is, whether the supremacy can be accounted for upon the sentimental hypothesis, explaining the nature of conscience.

how " authority is a constituent part of the idea"
of a mere feeling or desire. Or, at farthest, can
this, I would ask, be said in any other sense than
that in which any other feeling or desire has judgment, direction, superintendency, authority over
its own objects? Does not the sense of taste judge
and direct what food is to be taken, and superin-
tend the taking of food? has it not authority to
command one sort, forbid another?   Has the
moral sense authority in any other way than this
over its own objects? It is in vain to tell us of the
peculiar mental *position* which the moral faculty
occupies. The expression is a most just one, as
serving to convey the notion entertained by the
sentimentalists of the nature of the moral sense.
But surely our notion of this position does not inevitably imply, as something contained in that
notion, that *we ought* to gratify the faculty having
this position. To say that, while other faculties
have each their own objects, they are themselves
the objects of the moral faculty, may or may not
be good as a *reason* why we ought only to gratify
such of them as can be gratified with the agreeable, or without the painful emotion : but the
bare assigning of it as a reason, the assigning of
any sort of reason, the mere supposition that a
reason can be necessary, that a question can exist,
shews beyond all doubt that what we *ought* to do,
and what is *agreeable* to the moral faculty cannot
just mean one thing ; and if they do not mean one
thing, the theory is altogether untenable.

I have elsewhere asserted that precisely the same objection lies against the sentimental hypothesis, as against those theories which resolve right and wrong into the will of the Deity, or into human laws; to which I would now add, that there is no mode of defence that can possibly be adopted in behalf of the first, that may not be employed in behalf of the other two, with equal,— in my opinion, with greater plausibility. We are told, for instance, that all that we mean by an action's being right, is just this, that it is agreeable to the moral sense — " no notion can be formed of the moral faculty that does not comprehend authority, superintendence, direction." But is it not at least as rational to say, — all that we mean by an action's being right, is, that it is agreeable to the divine will, that it is in conformity to the laws of the land, — no notion can be formed of the divine will, of civil law, that does not comprehend authority, superintendence, direction? How could we treat assertions of this nature otherwise than by just pronouncing them to be entirely arbitrary and groundless? or could any consideration be urged against them that would not apply, with at least equal force, *mutatis mutandis*, to the assertions of the sentimental theorist?*

* To this I may add, that the same confusion seems to have existed, in fact, as regards the specific aims of those different theories. I know not very well whether those who have founded morality on the laws of God, or the laws of men, have

The only thing which has preserved the sentimental theory from the prompt and decided rejection met by the two opinions now alluded to, is the delusion occasioned by the ambiguity of the terms *moral sense* and *conscience*. Is man endowed with a moral sense?—undoubtedly. Is it by the moral sense that he judges of right and wrong?—most certainly. Can he distinguish right and wrong without a moral sense? — truly not. Ought not the moral sense to be the supreme guide of his conduct?—without question. What more, cry the sentimentalists, can any one desire? Nay, but it is overlooked that all this is true of the moral sense, only in its general meaning, as denoting the

meant that our perception of moral distinctions resolves into our knowledge, that some actions are commanded, others forbidden ; or that those actions which we perceive, no matter how, to be right or wrong, are those which are commanded or forbidden, by Divine or human authority — that is, whether they answer the question, how do *we* attach a moral distinction to certain qualities of actions? or this one, on account of what quality *in actions* is it, that we attach such moral distinction to them? But the confounding of these two questions really does not, in regard to any one more than another, of the theories now alluded to, arise from a defect in these theories, but from the mismanagement of them. For as, on the one hand, Sir James Mackintosh allows that the two questions have been confounded by some of the sentimentalists, so, on the other, it is clear, that they admit of being distinguished, on the other systems now compared with that. For, supposing that *right* and *wrong* mean just *commanded* and *forbidden*, we may still, separately, inquire for what *quality* certain actions have been commanded, others forbidden.

faculty, whatever it may be, by which right and wrong are distinguished ; and under which meaning the moral sense may really stand for the reasoning faculty. But all that is thus true of the moral sense, or conscience, in the *general signification of these terms*, the sentimentalists unconsciously represent as true of the moral sense, or conscience, as *specially denoting a capacity of receiving agreeable or disagreeable emotion* from the view of certain actions ; — hence, I repeat, the whole plausibility of their theory.

Upon the whole, then, in return for the dilemma which Sir James Mackintosh proposes to the intellectualists,* I would beg to offer the following one :—

If to perform such actions as excite the agreeable emotion, (the capacity of which and of its contrary is supposed to constitute the moral faculty,) is not something morally right or obligatory, something that it is our duty, or that we ought to do,—then it cannot be said that the moral faculty is what ought to be the guide of our conduct—which is absurd.

If to do such actions as excite the agreeable emotion, *is* something morally right, this is something which we must perceive to be morally right, otherwise than as it excites the agreeable emotion ; unless we merely mean to say, that doing what excites the agreeable emotion, excites the

---

* To this effect — If the emotion is denied, a known fact is denied : if admitted, what use for any other supposition ?

agreeable emotion. And, if we can perceive, otherwise than by the supposed capacity of emotion, that any one thing is right, why may we not perceive that any other thing is right, and what is the use of supposing the existence of that capacity at all ?

With regard to the theory, adopted by Sir James, which attempts to resolve the moral faculty into simpler component elements, by means of the principle of association, I have only to observe, that, as that theory at most proposes to explain a sentiment or emotive act, it can never, even supposing it true, be accepted by a disciple of the intellectual school, as furnishing an adequate or complete account of our moral perceptions. And although the existence of a sentiment, as a constituent part, or rather as the attendant of many of our determinations, is fully admitted by the intellectual theorist, yet as he pretends to account satisfactorily for the existence of the sentiment, as being a strictly necessary consequence, in cases where it occurs, of the previous intellectual perception ; he cannot admit that this sentiment may be wholly rested upon the principle of association. But as the existence of an intellectual perception, with its necessary attendant desires and emotions by no means excludes the possibility of other desires or emotions arising from other sources, coexisting or concurring with these moral emotions more strictly so denominated, a hypothesis which accounts for the existence of such auxiliary sentiments, as it is not necessary as a part of the intellectual theory, yet does not, in the slightest degree, impugn or contradict it; and may be accepted into its alliance, as forming a collateral branch of the subject. In fact it has never been sufficiently attended to, that the intellectual theory is of a positive more than of a negative or exclusive kind. Its supporters maintain this point absolutely—Reason, without any additional faculty but what is implied in the existence of reason itself, can perceive something to be right, something wrong; and though other faculties may exist, pointing to what is right, reason alone can determine what is right. They can easily admit a variety of principles, subsidiary to reason, *impelling* to what is right.

In the course of the *Dissertation*, much interesting and judicious remark as it contains, there is nothing more valuable than the considerations incidentally urged to evince the supreme excellence of virtue, as regards the happiness of the agent; and the great amount of the happiness derived from the exercise of virtue, as independent of, and distinct from its fruits. No topic is more worthy to engage the attention of a philosophical and virtuous mind; and the manner in which it has been treated by the author of the Dissertation, evinces that the power of virtue is what he has alike deeply meditated upon, and warmly felt. And it would be with any design but that of controverting or weakening his observations — even if any thing I might be able to say could have that effect — that I should be inclined to object to the *theoretical* views, which I suppose they may be employed to serve. So long as the supreme happiness which virtue confers upon her votaries, is maintained as a fact; so long as the exhibition of this happiness is employed as the incentive to virtuous conduct, — no statement can be more just and important. But the theoretical principles which I have adopted, make me object to such representation's being used as explaining the nature of moral *obligation* — as if all that were meant by saying, this mode of conduct is your *duty*, were, this mode of conduct is that by which *you will secure your own greatest happiness.* It seems to me, however, that this is the only consistent, at least the most satisfactory, view of moral obligation, which a theorist of the sentimental school can propose. In opposition to this, it appears to me, that the happiness derived from the practice of virtue, instead of constituting obligation, presupposes its existence. I rejoice, I enjoy a felicity, in acting, or in having acted, or in proposing to act so, *because* I perceive such mode of acting to be my duty. It is only because I suppose it

K 2

my duty, that I feel joy in performing it, or that I could not dispense with the performance of it without uneasiness or remorse. The perception of duty is an intellectual act; the pleasure of doing, the pain of violating duty, an emotive act. This pleasure, conceived or desired, it is my *duty* to pursue or aim at, in the same sense as it is my duty to pursue or aim at any good of which my nature is capable: and if the enjoyment of this pleasure is my *supreme* good, the pursuit of it, so far as *duty to myself* goes, may be my *highest* duty. But this secondary duty, — secondary at least as regards the mode of its derivation — presupposes a primary duty, as before described: and this primary duty is not founded upon a view of a happiness to be enjoyed by myself, but is presupposed in the notion of this happiness. Other instances of obligations in a *series*, will occur in this treatise; and in cases where such series exists, philosophers have not always sufficiently distinguished between the first, and the following links of the chain. Something is, in its own nature, obligatory. Why? Because we find a happiness in doing it? — No; why then? We cannot tell, any more than we can tell why the whole must be greater than a part. It is, and must be obligatory: this is all we can say about the matter: and being obligatory, we must find a happiness in acting accordingly.

I would only add, that to rest the obligation of

virtue upon the happiness arising to the agent from its exercise, is really to adopt the selfish theory of morals, which Sir James so justly and earnestly opposes. Any other account of obligation which a sentimental theory can give, must, so far as I can see, have the effect of making *obligation* to mean nothing different from *inclination*.

CHAPTER IV.

VIEW OF THE ORIGIN AND NATURE OF OUR MORAL JUDGMENTS
AND FEELINGS, AND OF THE RELATED PRINCIPLES OF ACTION.

SECT. I.

Of Judgments and Feelings strictly Moral.

HAVING thus endeavoured to vindicate the agency
of reason in our moral determinations, I proceed
— with a view to ascertain how far the supposition of such agency is, of itself, sufficient to explain the phenomena — to exhibit the particular
modes and effects of its operation.

It is from the nature of pleasure and pain, happiness and misery, that all moral distinctions ultimately derive their origin : and as, among beings,
if such could be imagined to exist, whose condition admitted of no diversity in this respect, no
moral notions could possibly have birth; so,
wherever pain and pleasure are experienced, and
perceived to arise from the acts of animated beings, a variety of feelings, in relation to those two
states, and the beings who are the instruments of
producing them, will be the necessary result of a
certain degree of the capacity of thought and

knowledge; and in the minds of those beings who may possess such capacity expanded into the faculty of reason, there will also ensue, in regard to those objects of thought, a variety of *moral* determinations properly so denominated.

Of the various pleasures and pains incident to an intelligent being, some may be said to result from the very nature of mind ; others from the peculiar mental or bodily constitution, which it may have pleased the Creator to bestow. Of the first class, are the pleasures derived from the possession of knowledge, as opposed to ignorance or falsehood; from the possession of power; perhaps from that of the love and admiration of other beings: of the second class may be reckoned the emotions of taste, or at least some of those emotions ; and the whole class of our bodily pains and pleasures.

But however arbitrary, in some cases, may be the connection between our pleasures and pains, and the sources from which they are respectively derived, there is nothing arbitrary in the connection between those pleasures and pains, and the emotions of hope and fear, joy and sorrow, to which they severally give birth. Why the touch of a burning body should give us pain rather than pleasure, no reason can be given ; why certain sights, or tastes, or smells, should please rather than displease us, may perhaps be equally unaccountable : but it is impossible that a pleasure, obtained, or in prospect, should, as such, excite fear or sorrow, or *vice versa* with respect to pain. For we cannot even imagine a being, who should have the same feelings on being made to understand that he was about to undergo a great suffering, and to obtain a great enjoyment; or who should behold, with equal indifference, the approach of each. To say, as Dr. T. Brown has somewhere done, that " we know not why we have been so constituted by the Deity as to rejoice at prosperous, and grieve at unfortunate events," seems to me much the same as to say, that we know not why the Deity has made three and two to be equal to five; or the two sides of every triangle to be greater than the third.

Similar to the connection now described as subsisting between pleasure and pain and the emotions respectively related to each, is that between these states, and certain sentiments arising towards other beings, considered as the intentional producers of pleasure or pain. It is equally impossible for any being to be pleased with, or love another being, for causing him to endure pain, simply for the sake of doing so, as it is to be pleased with the pain itself, simply because it is such. It is impossible too that he should view the producer of pain, and the producer of pleasure, with similar sentiments, or with entire indifference in each case.

The principles of sympathy and benevolent affection towards other beings, do not, I apprehend, necessarily result from the nature of mind — at least of mind considered as unendued with *reason;* but if these principles have been implanted, the emotions of grief for the misery of others, joy on account of their happiness, love of those who benefit them, resentment towards those by whom they are injured, are not to be considered as what may or may not follow. Though the benevolent affections themselves may be merely the effect of positive constitution, the secondary emotions now enumerated flow of necessity from that constitution: for if I possess an affection towards another being, it is a contradiction to suppose that I could rejoice at his suffering, or that I could fail to grieve at such suffering, and resent the infliction of it.

Thus then we account for certain emotions which a view of the actions of other beings excite in our minds: and in doing so, we account for what very much resembles the sentiments of approbation and disapprobation, and what these sentiments are generally more or less mixed up with. Love to those who do us good, hatred to those who do us evil, are what must necessarily result from the very nature of mind. Love to those who do good to other beings for whom we entertain a benevolent affection, hatred towards those who injure them, are the necessary results of the possession of that affection.

There exists, then, in the very nature of mind, considered in its relation to the states of pleasure and pain, a necessary connection between these states and certain emotions peculiarly related to each. It is impossible to overlook the strong analogy, in kind, that subsists between these emotions and those of moral approbation and disapprobation; and we have thence the clearest warrant for forming the presumption, that, in the *essential nature of mind* also — mind in its higher and more developed capacities — we may find the source of moral perceptions in general.

Moral approbation has the closest possible affinity to hope, joy, gratitude; moral disapprobation to fear, grief, resentment. The former are all pleasing, the latter all painful emotions. Moral approbation, hope, joy, gratitude, have all a relation to pleasure or happiness as their object: with each of these emotions is more or less intermixed a feeling of love or desire. Moral disapprobation, fear, grief, resentment, have all a relation to pain or misery as their object: with each of these emotions again is more or less intermixed a feeling of hate or aversion. As surely then as any of these states of emotion have their origin in the essential nature of mind, so surely, we may presume, have the others; as surely as some of these emotions are not arbitrarily connected with their respective objects, so surely may we presume that none of them are arbitrarily connected.

A capability of the emotions of hope, joy, and gratitude, and their opposites, fear, grief, and resentment, does not seem to require a higher degree of intellect, than will enable a living being to *know* that pleasure or pain is inflicted, or about to be inflicted, and that by the act of another being. This degree, the lower animals seem to possess; and from their being endowed with certain benevolent affections towards their offspring, and sometimes with capacities of attachment or dislike towards other beings, they are necessarily pleased or displeased with those who benefit or injure the objects of those affections.

But an entirely new set of mental phenomena present themselves to our view, when we look to the case of a being endowed with *reason;* who is not merely capable of feeling pleasure and pain, and, when these are produced by the acts of other beings, of knowing that they are thus produced; but who can also think and reflect what pleasure and pain are, what is their distinctive nature, and thence, the distinctive nature of the different acts by which they are respectively produced.

The rational faculty may properly be said to consist in the ability, not merely to form a *conception* in the mind (for this must perhaps be allowed to the inferior animals) but to discover what any conception necessarily involves or contains in it. Every conception that a rational being can form, must inevitably involve or contain something within it. There must be something which cannot but hold true of it, as long as the conception remains the same; so that whenever this should not hold true, the conception itself would be changed or destroyed. The power of thus *evolving* a conception is the *reasoning faculty*—thé possession of which constitutes a rational being.

A being destitute of reason can behold, perceive, or know an object, as it is; but he cannot perceive what, according to the conception it gives birth to, must, with necessary truth, be affirmed or denied of it.* Thus a dog, or a horse, beholds and feels a stone, and knows its existence, as well as a man; but the former cannot, like the latter, deduce a necessary truth from his conception of it;—cannot, for instance, perceive that it is impossible for the stone at once to be, and not to be; that it cannot be in two places at one time; that all its parts are equal to the whole of it, and the like.

Pleasure and pain, happiness and misery, then, which, to the irrational creation, are at most but objects of knowledge or conception, or the exciting causes of certain passions or emotions, become besides, to the rational mind, the objects of thought and reasoning; and the conceptions formed of

* Whether reasoning can, or cannot be carried on without the instrumentality of language, is a point I am not at present concerned in determining. But I cannot here describe my meaning, without at least speaking of reasoning as what involves the use of language, in affirming or denying.

them in the reasoning mind, are perceived to involve such truths as these:

That they can only be, as states of a sentient being, and imply the existence of a sentient being:

That pleasure, in its very nature, and from the nature of a sentient being, must move joy, hope, desire; at least that the contrary of this cannot be. That pain must move grief, fear, resentment.

With these conceptions of what pain and pleasure are, and what they imply, the rational mind perceives farther, that pleasure is a state in which a sentient being *ought* to be, rather than in pain: that his being in a state of pleasure, or at least of ease, is *fit, right;* his being in a state of pain, *unfit, wrong;* and again, that an act which produces what is fit in regard to any sentient being, is an act which *ought* to be performed, or which an agent ought to perform—the performance of which is *right:* on the contrary, that an act which produces what, in regard to a sentient being, is unfit, ought not to be performed; is what an agent ought not to perform; what the performance of is *wrong*.

A rational being then does not merely, like the inferior animals, feel, or know pleasure or happiness, rejoice in it, desire it, and feel gratitude towards the agency by which it is produced; but he perceives that it is what, in its nature, must necessarily excite those passions: that it is the state in which he and every being *ought* to be, rather than in the contrary state: that an act which occasions

pleasure or happiness, ought to be performed, and
is right.   In like manner he does not merely feel
pain, grieve at being subjected to it, fear its approach, resent the act which inflicts it; but he
perceives that it is the natural and necessary cause
of grief, fear, resentment; that it is what ought
not to be occasioned; that the acts by which it is
occasioned, ought not to performed, and are wrong.
This then is *reasoning* * from the nature of pleasure and pain, or happiness and misery, and of
these as occasioned by the acts of an agent; and
the truths involved in the conception of these objects, form the *first principles of moral science.*

A being then who is incapable of reasoning from
the conceptions of his mind, of perceiving what
these conceptions contain or involve, is incapable
of perceiving a moral truth, of forming a moral
notion.   On the other hand, a being who is capable of reasoning, must be capable of forming moral determinations — unless we can suppose a
capacity of reasoning on one subject, as disjoined
from a similar capacity in regard to another subject.   All this seems incontestably true in theory:
certainly nothing to the contrary can be shewn

---

* *Reasoning* generally means the deduction of one proposition from *another:* but the making out of the first and primary
proposition, if a necessary intuitive truth, is reasoning from the
conception denoted by the terms it employs.   Thus the axiom,
" the whole is greater than a part," is produced by reasoning
from our conceptions of *whole* and *part.*

from fact.   Every rational being is a moral being
—every moral being is a rational being.

Let us now observe the order in which our moral judgments proceed.

The first principle in morals seems to be that
which has been derived from the very conception
we form of pleasure and pain, happiness and
misery, and of a sentient existence of which these
are the states : namely, that *it is fit that every sentient being should be happy rather than miserable.*

The notion of *fitness* next involves that of *obligation.*   It is impossible to perceive that something
is, *in itself*, fit to be done, without perceiving also
that it is what *an agent ought to do* — what he is
under an obligation to do, rather than the contrary,
and *vice versa.*

It seems impossible, in like manner, to have the
notion of an agent's being *under an obligation* to
do this, or to avoid doing that, without perceiving
it to be fit, in consequence, that *his state* should
be *better* if he *chooses* to do what is obligatory,
than if he does not ; worse, if he chooses to do
what it is obligatory to avoid, than if he chooses to
avoid it.   For it appears a contradiction to say
that a man is under an obligation to do something,
and yet that he ought to be no better or worse,
whether his choice be to do it or not.

So far there may be said to take place, a mere
intellectual perception of certain truths, which a
rational being finds to be involved in some of the

conceptions of his understanding. On considering the nature of the truths thus perceived, however, the perception of them must appear to be necessarily attended, as regards the mind of the percipient being, with the following consequences.

First, If he perceives that a thing is *fit to be done*, he must feel some *wish or desire* that it should be done — must have some pleasure or satisfaction in its being done, rather than the contrary.

Secondly, If he feels a wish that something should *be done*, he must feel some wish or desire *to do* it.

Thirdly, If he perceives that it is obligatory upon him to do something, he must feel some wish to fulfil the obligation; and this, *as an obligation*, and independently of the fitness of the *effect* taken by itself.

Fourthly, He must feel some complacency or affection towards any being who desires or wills to do what is fit or obligatory; and a certain satisfaction with himself, when conscious of such desire or will — and *vice versa* in each case.

Now this *disposition* of a rational mind to feel satisfaction or pleasure at the production of fit effects; this desire to be instrumental in producing them, and to fulfil the obligation perceived to result from their being fit; this complacency in the display of similar dispositions in the minds of other beings, and affection towards such beings,

this — for it is all one principle — is *moral virtue.*
In whatever degree an agent is under the influence of such principle, as a general character of his mind, he is a virtuous agent; and in every particular instance in which he actually experiences the satisfaction which a view of the production of fit effects is calculated to afford him, or in which he conceives admiration or attachment towards another virtuous agent, he exercises *moral approbation.* In explaining then what *virtue* is in itself, in its nature and origin, we explain what *approbation* * is, what is its nature and origin. The one thing involves the other: the one is but the other manifested or excited in a particular mode. To approve virtue, and to have virtue, are the same thing; for the one cannot be without the other.†

In developing the origin and nature of virtue and of moral approbation, it has seemed advisable, in the first instance at least, to represent them as in the mind of *one agent.* In pursuing the investigation, however, it is more convenient to

* i. e. So far as approbation is merely an *emotion.*

† That is, *absolutely* speaking, and so far as regards the nature of the principle: for when, in ordinary language, we say that a man has virtue, we speak relatively; and mean that he is virtuous in a considerable degree, or that his virtue is perfect, so far as human virtue is generally found to be. In short, I say that he who approves virtue is virtuous, in the same sense as I should say, that there is a fire, where there is a spark.

follow the common mode of separating the agent into two capacities : placing ourselves in one, as the approving or disapproving spectators ; the agent himself in the other, as the virtuous or vicious subject who excites those emotions. Accommodating our phraseology then to this mode of stating the case, we may be said to have been explaining, first, *why* certain *ends* are *fit*, certain *actions obligatory ; how* certain *individuals* are *virtuous* or *of good desert; how* they come to be so, and *wherein* their virtue or desert consists : and secondly, why and how *we judge* that such ends are fit, that such actions are obligatory, that such individuals deserve reward ; why *we are pleased* to see fit ends effected, why *we approve* of those actions by which they are sought to be effected : in other words, we explain, at once, wherein moral distinctions consist, and how we come to perceive them.

That the various emotions and affections now described must arise, of necessity, from the nature of the judgments to which they have been traced, seems indisputably clear. When a rational being perceives as a truth, by his reason, that something is right to be done, it is impossible for him to feel an entire *indifference* as to whether that be done or not : as impossible to be pleased at its not being done, or displeased at its being done. In like manner, if there is any thing that he is thus pleased to see done, he must be pleased

with the one who desires or seeks to do it. He
cannot be satisfied with the *effect*, dissatisfied with
the intending *producer* of that effect. Now it is
to be observed that this representation does not
suppose any *implanted* susceptibility or faculty,
additional to mere life and intelligence. The affections and emotions described are strictly necessary consequences of the mere intellectual perception of right and wrong ; as strictly so, as the
equality of the halves is the necessary consequence of the equality of the wholes which those
halves compose. The very notion of *right* carries
along with it that it is what we *must desire to be
done*, and cannot fail to desire ; and it would be a
contradiction to say that we could think any thing
to be right, and yet be entirely indifferent whether
it were done or not ; or regard in the same manner him who does what is right, and him who
does not.

The observation of Bishop Butler, that the
moral faculty includes "both a perception of the
understanding and a sentiment of the heart,"
though, in a general sense, conveying the substance of the foregoing statement, would require,
before it could be taken as fully expressing the
views therein contained, to be attended with the
following explanations :

First, That the popular expression "the heart,"
is not to be held as necessarily implying any principle distinct from, or superadded to, the pos-

session of a rational mind. I say *necessarily* implying : for I am not concerned to argue against the possibility, or even the fact, of an *implanted* and positive capacity of emotion,* as connected with the view of particular actions. It is sufficient for me to maintain that the existence of certain emotions can be accounted for, without the supposition of any such positive constitution ; that they may be shewn to arise from the mere possession of intelligence, and cannot but arise where there is intelligence.

But secondly, and more particularly, — That though, when a right or wrong action is really performed, there is both a perception of the understanding and a sentiment of the heart, yet, as we can determine an action to be right or wrong without its being performed at all, and therefore (since the emotion only takes place in relation to the performance) without any emotion, — the emotion has no share whatever, in determining it to be right or wrong.

The opinion that reason discriminates between right or wrong has suffered considerably from its having been the practice of theorists to confine their speculations on this subject exclusively to what takes place in our minds when an action is *performed*. Now we can just as clearly judge

---

* Dr. Price seems disposed to admit the existence of this capacity as superadded to reason.

that one action is right, another wrong, without their being actually performed, as we can judge that all the parts are equal to the whole, without making the experiment of dividing material bodies and reuniting the parts. Talk, as an abstract case, of inflicting pain or misery in any living being : on merely understanding what this means we pronounce the action wrong. This is a *moral* determination perfect in itself; and it is quite unmixed with emotion. We behold this wrong action *performed*, and we then feel a painful emotion because the *wrong* action is *performed*. If we have thought of it before performance, the act of judgment has taken place by itself;* if only upon seeing the performance, the act of judgment is immediately followed by the emotion; the emotion takes full possession of the mind, and we are apt to overlook the judgment : but the judgment, the judgment alone, is the *distinctive* operation ;† the emotion is but consequent upon the perception of the distinction.

* The *desire* to perform or avoid performance of an action perceived to be good or bad (or the desire that it should be performed or avoided by another agent) though it is what must take place *before* the action is performed, has always relation to the actual performance, and only springs up where actual performance *is likely, or at least possible.* The judgment that an action is right or wrong, may be formed regarding an action the actual performance of which is impossible.

† Let me not be taken as meaning, by the *distinctive* operation, that which distinguishes the primary quality of the action

A man hears that a particular occurrence has taken place, which, though he is not directly affected by it, he perceives will be, in its consequences, extremely prejudicial to him : he pronounces it an *unfortunate* occurrence, and feels much *regret* that it has happened.   In this case, his contemplation of the occurrence includes both "a perception of the understanding and a sentiment of the heart."   But surely the sentiment or emotion of regret has nothing to do in characterizing the occurrence as *unfortunate*.   He could have pronounced that it would be unfortunate without its happening at all — of course without any sentiment of regret, and also without any sentiment of fear, if the occurrence had been unlikely to happen.   It is not unfortunate because of his regret, nor does his regret attend the perception that it is unfortunate—as that perception exists by

for which it is determined to be right or wrong. This is a separate act from both of those which I have described, and precedes both. It is generally neither emotion nor judgment, in the strict sense, (though judgment may sometimes be employed) but perception or knowledge. I see a man receive a wound from another. This is the action. I perceive or know that it creates pain and inconvenience. This is the quality of the action which makes it the subject of a moral judgment. Reason pronounces that, as inflicting pain, the action is wrong. The actual *performance* of this *wrong* action moves in me a painful emotion.

The instinctive feeling of pity or compassion again is different from all those, and what we have here no concern with.

itself; the feeling of regret arises because what is perceived to be *unfortunate—has happened.*

A man's judgment that an action is morally good or bad — his judgment that an event will have consequences beneficial or prejudicial to himself — are, as judgments, entirely different. But in the manner in which each is attended with an emotion, in the manner in which each exists independently of that emotion — they are precisely similar.

It is at all events to be observed — in extension of Bishop Butler's analysis, — that neither the judgment, nor the emotion, of which the act of moral approbation consists, is one, or indivisible, but each twofold. We *judge*, first, that an *effect* is *fit*, secondly, that an *action* is *obligatory*. We feel an *emotion*, first of, *satisfaction*, at the view of a fit *effect*, secondly, of *attachment* and admiration, towards a virtuous *agent*.

Our perception that an agent is under an obligation to do any thing, must presuppose that something is, in itself, fit to be done. The judgment of the understanding in each case precedes the affection or emotion; or that affection or emotion is not *moral approbation*. *I morally approve* that the end or effect should be produced, only when I have *judged* that it is fit and proper to be produced; and my moral approbation of the *agent* on account of his *virtue*, presupposes that there was something, in my judgment and his, perceived to be *obligatory,* in a regard to which his virtue consisted.

Of the Natural Affections.

Along with that regard to *moral fitness and obligation* which constitutes *virtue,* and which must, in some degree, however small, belong to every intelligent being, man possesses several benevolent desires or affections, by which he is directly impelled to promote the happiness of other beings, and to relieve their misery. These affections correspond so entirely, in some instances, with the principle of virtue, that some of the best writers have taken them for the same. Nothing however can be more different.

Some benevolent affections are general, as sympathy or compassion; some particular, as filial, and parental love : but all of them are mere desires, not having any necessary relation to their particular objects, but of a kind which we could easily suppose, at least, to be connected with other objects. We desire to render such a one happy, to relieve another from being miserable, and we act accordingly; not having in view any *fitness* in the effect that is to be produced; we merely desire it : we might have desired the contrary in each case ; and should as readily and naturally have sought to gratify the one desire, as the other. It is with these desires as with our desire of food, which is quite independent of any view to the support of life, and would of itself equally impel us to swallow poison as wholesome victuals, did they chance to be equally agreeable to the taste. But when we act as virtuous agents, the case is quite different; and we promote happiness, and relieve misery, because it is *fit* or *right* that such should be done, and not merely because we desire it. It is true such desire exists; but it does not exist primarily, or by positive constitution; but in necessary connection with the object, as conceived by a rational mind. If we desire such effect to take place, it is only because it appears to be, in its own nature, a *fit* effect: one which is naturally proper to be desired, and would not cease to be fit, even should we possess contrary desires. Did we not desire it, indeed, we should not promote it; but did it not, in our judgment, possess an intrinsic fitness, we should not even desire it.

Happiness and misery, as exciting the mere natural affections, are in the mind, not as objects of reason, but of sense or imagination. In vain you tell me that thousands lie dead or wounded in the field, or are perishing by shipwreck, by the earthquake, or the pestilence. I may hear all this, and comprehend what it means, and yet my feelings of compassion remain unmoved. But let me behold the agonies, let me hear the groans of a single sufferer; nay, fill my imagination with the vivid conception of them, and my heart is melted with sympathy and compassion. **Reason** and virtue, on the other hand, need not to be presented with either the reality, or the representation of misery. The bare conception of it formed in the intellect, is that of something which ought not to be, — which ought to be removed; and the desire and purpose of removing it instantly and necessarily follows. Hence, feeling is moved by the case of distress that is present, more than by thousands of cases that are future or absent; virtue is moved by the intrinsic importance of this or that amount of suffering, without relation to time or place. Feeling looks merely to the fact that there is suffering: it regards not the desert of the sufferer: it regards not whether he endures more than his due share, or whether his burden can be at all removed, without pressing harder upon another. It interests us alike in what befals the murderer and his victim: we forget the fate of the latter, when we behold the suffering endured by the former, in expiation of his crime. To the eye of reason and virtue, the view of suffering is always painful; but they can look, comparatively unmoved, on suffering deservedly inflicted, if it is the means of preventing other suffering, that would be undeserved: they are not satisfied that a present suffering is removed, if a greater is thereby created elsewhere, or in future; or if it is removed from one to another, who is already bearing what in justice belongs to him.

The difference between acting from a principle of virtue, and acting from the impulse of a benevolent affection, may be shewn in a variety of instances. A judge on the bench feels the strongest compassion (which is a benevolent affection) for a criminal: yet he condemns him from a sense of duty. It may be said, this sense of duty is itself a benevolent affection towards those who would suffer by the escape of the criminal. That this name may be given to it without any great impropriety, I shall allow: but are the two things the same? Does the judge feel an impulse of emotion, a feeling, a desire, towards those whom he benefits by passing sentence on the criminal? No; he acts in their behalf from a rational sense of moral obligation. The circumstance of his doing violence to his feelings in condemning the criminal, shews that it is something different from feeling or affection, that determines his conduct. Is a revenue officer prompted by benevolent affection in exacting government dues? Who are the objects of this affection? his superiors in his peculiar department? the public in general? Surely to say so would be an abuse of words.

A man gives his assistance to a scheme for the saving of human lives, such as the maintaining of a life-boat, the procuring of an apparatus for the recovery of persons apparently drowned, and the like, from a sense of duty: he acts with a view to prevent certain misfortunes to some of his fellow-men, as an *end*, right or fit to be pursued, and which he would not pursue, but because it is right. But let him behold a person actually about to sink under water; let him witness his agonizing struggles, and hear his screams of affright and horror, as he is swallowed up by the devouring flood — does he now seek to rescue the drowning man, because he perceives it to be *right?* No more than the drowning man seeks to rescue himself, because it is right. The efforts of the spectator to afford relief, are as instantaneous and violent as those of the sufferer to obtain it. The desire which agitates the one, seems equal to that which agitates the other. Both are alike moved by a sudden instinctive impulse, and by nothing else.

Brute animals display the very strongest degrees of benevolent affection : yet we never attribute to them the possession of moral excellence, or consider them as acting from a regard to moral duty. It would be absurd to say that I possess any affection towards any particular inhabitant of Lapland, or Japan; yet I would not for an instant hesitate to say, that it is right such a one should be happy, rather than miserable; nor could I, by any possible means, make myself to consider it as a matter of indifference, which of these two states he should be made to exist in; neither, if the event depended upon myself, could I for a moment doubt about ordering it in one way, rather than in the other. We can conceive beings not only destitute of benevolent affection, but actuated by feelings of malevolence, and deriving gratification from the infliction of suffering: we cannot conceive any who should think the infliction of suffering *right*, and be pleased with it as being so.

It seems impossible that, as rational and moral beings, we can attribute an excellence or worthiness to moral virtue, and feel an attachment towards those who are possessed of it, without a corresponding notion of excellence, a corresponding attachment, as regards the case of the benevolent affections. So far as relates to the mere production of fit effects, virtue and affection are the same: so far as the emotion of approbation consists in the satisfaction arising from the view of a fit effect, taken by itself, the results of virtue, and of benevolent affection, present to it the same object. Whether the parent protects and nourishes his child from duty, or from natural affection, the protection and nourishment are afforded: a sensitive being receives comfort and enjoyment: this is fit; and, as such, must be pleasing and agreeable to us. And as being each respectively dispositions, or propensions of an agent, tending to produce such fit effects, virtue and natural affection must, each in its own way, appear proper to excite our attachment towards it. Still our estimation of both cannot be alike. And of the two, moral virtue cannot fail to appear the most dignified and valuable. It is the attribute exclusively of a rational mind: it is a regard for what things are intrinsically, and in their nature, worthy of regard; and which are therefore regarded, because they are thus worthy. Benevolent affection, on the other hand, is a blind instinctive impulse; generally desiring what is fit to be desired, but not for that cause, nor for any cause: the desire exists in fact; and this is all we can say. Nor is it what is fit on the whole, that always results from the obeying of such desire. It is often but a fitness, partial, insulated, exclusive. One object is simply kept in view, simply pursued, without regard to the consequence which its attainment may draw along with it. — Virtue is essential to reason and intellect: they are co-existent: as long as reason stands, virtue must stand: nothing can eradicate the principle of virtue, that does not overturn the structure of reason, and dissolve the very constitution of the intelligent mind. Natural affection is a mere appendage, having no necessary connection with one nature more than with another, nor with any nature at all. It may exist in a brute, and be wanting in a seraph. It may burn bright to-day, and be extinguished to-morrow. It may be exchanged for its opposite, and become cruelty and malevolence; and yet the essential nature of the being who has possessed it, that in which the species of his being consists, may remain the same.

The one, in short, is a nature; the other, an accident: the one, fixed and unchangeable; the other, capricious and moveable.

But though thus inferior in excellence to moral virtue, the benevolent affections still appear to us to possess a comparative excellence, and excite a comparative attachment; and the want of them is viewed as a capital defect. In some respects indeed, they appear to possess a superiority in value over virtue itself, — virtue, however, be it remembered, calculated only according to the human standard. Our virtue is weak, our affections strong; we concede a value to the degree, which we should refuse to allow to the kind. Indeed our virtue, as it is, and without our affections, would go but a very short way in maintaining the happiness, or even preserving the existence, of mankind. In proportion as it embraces a wider range of objects, its operation, in regard to each, is more cold and languid. By being diffused, it is attenuated. Distracted by a variety of objects, it can rest on none. Intent on what is best, it misses what is good. Affection, on the contrary, sees, comparatively speaking, but one object; its power is concentrated upon it alone; it rushes towards it with unchecked impetuosity. If it is heedless of other objects, it at least attains that: if better ones are missed, still that is secured; nay, if better ones are counteracted, still all is not lost. Virtue is slow, timid, cautious, calcu-

lating; affection is prompt, decisive, eager, pre-
cipitate.

This exclusiveness and particularity of the *affections*, and consequent concentration of their warmth
on a single object, is the cause why we are so
much more gratified and pleased, when others act
towards us from affection, than when they are
moved merely by a sense of duty. " A benefactor
thinks himself but ill requited, if the person upon
whom he has bestowed his good offices, repays
them merely from a cold sense of duty, and without any affection to his person. A husband is dissatisfied with the most obedient wife, when he
imagines her conduct is animated by no other
principle, besides her regard to what the relation
she stands in requires. Though a son should fail
in none of the offices of filial duty, yet if he wants
that affectionate reverence which it so well becomes him to feel, the parent may justly complain
of his indifference. Nor could a son be quite satisfied with a parent, who, though he performed
all the duties of his situation, had nothing of that
fatherly fondness which might have been expected
from him." (Smith's Theory of Mor. Sent. Part 3.
ch. 6.) — Not only are the actual services of
affection more valuable, from the greater zeal
which prompts them; but the pleasure we feel in
being the objects of this zeal, is more flattering
and delightful, than what we experience in being
viewed with the colder, and more general interest

which virtue inspires. It is not enough that we are absolutely loved; we must be loved exclusively, or more than others: nor do we care for being the objects of a regard, which, unless our deserts give us a right to it, is equally bestowed on every other being.

The distinction between the virtuous principle and the benevolent affections, is of no mean consequence to be observed; and many perplexities have been introduced into the theory of morals, from the circumstance of its being overlooked. It is not perhaps going too far to say, that there is not a greater difference — in the case of a man's doing good to himself — between his eating from appetite, and his doing so in order to gain strength and preserve life, when indisposition may have removed the relish for food, than— in the case of his doing good to others — between acting from a benevolent affection, and from virtue. Hunger is a bodily, parental or filial love, a mental affection: in other respects they act with entire similarity.

It was before observed, that it is impossible, in the nature of things, to possess a benevolent affection towards any being, and not be pleased with such actions as promote his happiness, displeased with the contrary. These feelings however must never be identified with moral approbation and disapprobation, taken in their proper meaning; to which they bear only the same relation that instinctive gratitude and resentment do, (i. e. gratitude for an enjoyment bestowed, or a pain inflicted, on *self;*) the susceptibility of which does not even suppose the capacity of reason. A brute *resents* an attack upon its young, but cannot be said to *disapprove* of it.

SECT. III.

Of the precise Sense in which Approbation and Disapprobation are Acts of Reason.

We shall now be able to estimate, with some degree of precision, how far, and in what sense, approbation and disapprobation can properly be termed *acts of reason;* or reason the power that distinguishes right from wrong.

The meaning of the terms *approbation* and *disapprobation* has been occasionally so far extended, as to comprehend every species of judgment, emotion, or affection, which a view of the acts, character, or disposition of living agents, may excite in us. In like manner, the terms *good* and *bad* often include, besides the moral notions of obligatory, virtuous, and meritorious, every character or quality of a living being, that can in any way move our affection or dislike. Of course we have found it necessary to distinguish the various species of mental acts or states, to which the names of approbation and disapprobation are, or might be applied; and to make a similar distinction of the corresponding objects of these sentiments.

Now it has appeared, that the feelings of gratitude and resentment, respectively, for favours or injuries done to us, or those to whom we bear affection, do not imply any exercise of reason: these emotions being exhibited, on such occasions, by living creatures whom it is not usual to consider as being endowed with reason.

We have endeavoured to make it appear, however, that beings endowed with reason, and furnished with the occasions that give birth to moral conceptions, must perceive certain general truths, such as these :—that happiness ought to be promoted rather than misery : that what in itself ought to be done, an agent ought to do : that an agent who chooses to do what he ought, ought to be rewarded accordingly. So far as this is admitted, the agency of reason, in discriminating right and wrong, can of course admit of no controversy.

When an agent performs, or is desirous to perform, that which is obligatory upon him, we say he is a *good* agent, or a *virtuous* agent, or his action is morally *good*, or *virtuous*. Now these are not propositions, but definitions. To affirm such things, is certainly not an act of reasoning, any more than it is an act of reasoning to say, that a figure of three sides and three angles is a triangle. We do not then, in such a sense as this, distinguish what is morally good or bad by reason.

Again, when we say that any particular moral

agent is a good moral agent, or the contrary,—
as that the Deity is good; that Howard was
good; that Nero was bad; we assert mere propositions of fact. Such propositions are not discovered by reason: they do not belong to morals
as a science, any more than the proposition, —
the earth is spherical, — is a truth discovered by
reason,* or one belonging to the science of mathematics.

But whether we assert, in general, that certain
species of characters and actions are good, or that
particular characters or actions are of that species;
in either case, we presuppose a judgment of reason: namely, that something is fit or obligatory—
in the performance of which, goodness is defined
to consist: and which goodness, so defined or understood, we ascribe to particular characters or
actions.

It has been farther stated, however, that what
reason perceives as fit to be done, must necessarily give some species of satisfaction to the mind
of the reasoning being, when he beholds it done;
and also that he must necessarily be moved with
a certain attachment and admiration towards the
agent. Now most certainly the emotions which
are thus generated on beholding the performance
of certain actions, are not acts of reason, in the
proper or usual meaning of that expression; and
so far as these emotions are constituent parts of

* That is, by *reasoning* a priori, from intuitive principles.

the sentiments * of approbation and disapprobation, and, as such, distinctive of right and wrong,
so far it may be correct to say, that the moral faculty is something different from reason.   But although it is not maintained that nothing else than
a bare judgment of the understanding takes place,
when we determine the moral character of an action which we behold performed ; it is maintained
that such a judgment does take place; that when
we call an action right or wrong, we do not mean
only to declare, as a fact, that we have a certain
feeling, but are under a persuasion that to such
an action, this feeling, and no other, is suitable;
and that, not only in regard to our constitution,
but in the nature of things.   And finally, it is
maintained, that even to represent *reason* as the
sole judge of right and wrong, is what admits of
entire justification, both in propriety of language,
and in point of fact ;   since the emotions themselves that arise on the view of different moral
actions, are not the result of any principle of our
nature *separate from reason*, but are the necessary
and unavoidable effect of the mere possession of
life and intelligence.

The *emotion* is not *reasoning*, but a *state of a
reasoning mind;* what a reasoning mind must be
liable to exist in, if conversant with happiness
and misery, and conceiving of actions productive

* This is a convenient term, as being applicable both to the
judgment and the *feeling.*

of the one or the other. It must fear, hope, joy, sorrow, love, hate, approve, disapprove. It must be pleased with truth and knowledge, displeased with ignorance and deceit. What we say, in short, is this :—grant us *reason*, and we account for approbation, both as a *judgment*, and an *emotion*. Whether the emotion is to be reckoned an act of reason, is a question of words. On the other hand, we grant you the *emotion*, and say that you cannot, with it alone, explain the phenomena sought to be explained.

The capacity of any species of feeling or emotion whatever, seems to be considered, by some philosophers, as a sort of appendage to a rational mind, which it might have existed without, in the same way as our bodies could subsist, without this or that particular limb or organ. To me, I confess, this appears very nearly the same as to talk of the principle of life, as of a component part of our being, separate from reason; or to speak of extension as something separate from figure, though generally found added to it. To suppose a being endowed with reason, subject to pleasure and pain, and conceiving others as subject to them,—to suppose that such a being could be *without* desires or aversions, hopes or fears, joys or sorrows, appears to me as absurd as to suppose he may have reason without life, or that matter may have impenetrability without extension. The love and admiration, then, which we bear towards virtuous actions and characters, is not like any of our animal desires, affections, or propensities,—which seem to be of an arbitrary kind,—but is a necessary result of the nature of a rational mind, and of the nature of virtue, considered as an object of conception to that mind.

In the same way as the mere possession of a rational nature accounts for our approbation of moral virtue in an agent, it accounts for our approbation of what may be styled amiable qualities, such as the benevolent affections, general and particular. It cannot admit of doubt that it is from their relation to the promotion of happiness that these qualities derive their excellence; and that this excellence must be discovered and valued by every rational being, who, perceiving the fitness of happiness as an end, must necessarily be pleased with all those dispositions that tend to promote it.

I may now take occasion to observe, that many of the most plausible objections to the *reasoning* hypothesis have existence solely in a neglect of discriminating the different parts of the complex act which we term *approbation:* a term of complex meaning, even in its strictest usage,—still more so in the popular application of it. I *approve* of an act, when I am simply *pleased* with it, as being beneficial to myself or to some one whom I regard with affection; and this without any consideration of its *moral* character. I *approve* of it, when I *judge* it to be, in itself, fit to be performed. I *approve* of it, when I *judge* the agent, rather than any other person, to be under a peculiar obligation to perform it. I *approve* of it, when I make these *judgments* respecting it, before it is performed. I *approve* of it, when I experience an agreeable *emotion* in beholding it performed. I *approve* of it, though it was neither what the agent was particularly bound to perform, nor even in itself fit to be performed, if he has merely performed it with a good *intention*. I *approve* of it, if the agent has executed this intention at the cost of doing *violence to himself*, quite otherwise than I should have done, had it been altogether according to his inclination. I *approve* of it, if the agent has merely acted from the impulse of a natural affection, in so far as that affection moves my attachment and sympathy.

Mr. Hume, speaking of the hypothesis which ascribes the moral perceptions to reason, expresses himself as follows :

"It is impossible that, in any particular instance, this hypothesis can so much as be rendered intelligible, whatever specious figure it may make in general declamations and discourses. Examine the crime of ingratitude, for instance, which has place wherever we observe good will expressed and known, together with good offices performed, on the one side, and a return of ill-will or indifference, with ill offices or neglect, on the other. Anatomize all these circumstances, and examine, by your reason alone, in what consists the demerit or blame. You never will come to any issue or conclusion. Reason judges either of matter of fact or of relations. Inquire then, first, where is the matter of fact which we here call crime; point it out; determine the time of its existence; describe its essence or nature."—" Does the morality consist in the relation of its parts to each other? How? after what manner? specify the relation. Be more particular and explicit in your propositions, and you will easily see their falsehood."

This passage may be given as a fair sample of the way in which the different moral qualities of actions, as for instance the *obligation* of the *action*, and the *virtue* of the *agent*, have generally been confounded together. Does Mr. Hume here make reference to the ungrateful disposition, as something in the mind of the agent; or to the obligation or duty lying on that agent, whatever his individual disposition might be? or, which of these soever he may have in view, what is the *proposition*, the affirmation, regarding ingratitude, that we are called to consider? " Examine the crime of ingratitude" — Examine, one might as well say, the figure called a triangle. Is the triangle, one might ask, a relation or a matter of fact? — But without meeting in detail the somewhat captious, and not always intelligible challenges here offered, I would at once state, that to ascribe blame or demerit to ingratitude, may be to affirm one or other or all of these propositions :

First. *An agent* who has received kindness from any being, *ought not to do hurt* to that being in return :

Second. An agent who does what he ought not to do, in hurting one who has benefited himself, is an *ungrateful* or *morally bad* agent :

Third. Such an agent *deserves punishment* for his ungrateful conduct :

Fourth. *We view* such an agent with *dislike* and *resentment*.

Now I am prepared to shew that the first and third of these propositions are strictly deducible from one or more *intuitive truths discovered by reason ;* and this, in relation to the present instance, is all that the advocates of reason would maintain : the second is simply a *definition :* the fourth may be allowed, though it is not so, to be mere matter of fact. But did not reason perceive the truth of the first affirmation, the others would never have been formed.

It occurs to me also to mention here, that Mr. Hume, somewhere in his works, finds an argument for the truth of the theory which he espouses, in this circumstance, that, while in speaking on other subjects, such as reason is cognizant of, we employ, as the *copula* of our propositions, some part of the verb *to be—is, was, will be,—*we, on the contrary, whenever we introduce a moral notion, must adopt the word *ought,* or some other quite different from the verb *to be.* — On this I would merely observe, that the use of the verb *to be* takes place as much in morals, when we say *is* right, *is* wrong, as when we say, in mathematics, *is* equal, *is* unequal; and that the expression, *ought* to be, expressing fitness or obligation, is not more remote from the mere indicative mood of the substantive verb, than is the expression, *may be,* expressing possibility; or *must be,* expressing necessity. Indeed the three several notions of *what may be,*—*what must be,*—*what ought to be,*—carry, on the face of them, so plain an appearance of belonging to one family, that stronger grounds would seem to be required for attributing them to different origins, than merely (the only plausible ground assigned) that we feel a *satisfaction* when what *ought* to be done *is* done—a satisfaction not experienced—from the difference of their specific nature—in regard to either of the other perceptions.

CHAPTER V.

RECAPITULATION — ANALYSIS OF THE COMPLEX NOTION OF A MORAL ACTION.

WITH the preceding section terminated the discussion of the first of the two questions stated at the outset, as forming the principal divisions of the present inquiry, or that which relates to the nature of the moral faculty. The discussion of the second is now to be entered upon — to which the remaining chapters of this *Part* are but preliminary.

It has already appeared, however, that we must treat this question not as asking simply—wherein does the goodness of an action consist, but wherein does its fitness, its obligation, its virtue, its merit consist.

We have seen that, when we come to analyze the notion of an action in morals, we find it to be a complex one, separable into several different parts. There is, in the first place, an *effect* produced by such action — a sentient being, the object of the action, receiving pain or pleasure from it; or, if there are more than one object, the pain or pleasure distributed in particular proportions to each. This *effect* viewed by itself, and without any regard whatsoever to the character, conduct, or intention of an *agent*, nay even though we suppose it produced by a blind undesigning cause, we judge to be *fit* or *unfit* to take place. That any being should be happy rather than miserable; that, if there are more than one, a pleasure should be shared by all rather than enjoyed by one, is what we are pleased with in itself. So far the action, i. e. the effect of it, is *fit*. Obligation is a certain *state*, situation, or condition, in which an agent is placed *in relation* to this effect: he is under an *obligation* to produce the effect: there exists a certain reason or cause why he should produce it. No ideas can be more dissimilar than that of an effect or end, fit in itself to be produced, and that of the relative situation of an agent, who is bound or ought to produce it. We can conceive different agents to be each under a different degree of obligation to produce an effect of the same fitness. Among agents similarly situated, the fitness of the effect of an action is the measure of its obligation; but the obligation does not depend on this alone. The same effects, considered as *proper* to an action, will follow the performance of that action, whether the agent has promised to perform it or not; but it may be, in the highest degree, obliga-

tory on him in the one case, not at all in the other.
The estimate of obligation then is formed upon a
conjunct view of the fitness of the effect, and the
situation or circumstances of the agent in relation
to the subject of the action. Again; different
agents under equal degrees of obligation, may be
conceived as differently disposed to the fulfilment
of it. *Virtue* then is a character, nature, or quality
of an *agent's mind or disposition,* by which he is
more or less sensible to the influence of the motive
which obligation furnishes. The idea of this *character* or quality of the agent's mind, which we call
his *virtue,* is as different from that of the situation
or relative position in which he stands with regard
to the production of a certain effect, (which state
we call his being under an obligation,) as the idea
of this state of obligation is different from that of
the useful or hurtful effects of the action. And
in like manner as, where the fitness of the effect
is equal, the obligation on each of two agents may
be different; so, where obligation may be the
same, the virtue, the sensibility to that obligation
may be different in different agents. Farther,
where two agents are both under the same obligation, and naturally formed with equal degrees of
regard to its influence, we can conceive one, by a
voluntary *effort of free will,* (which we must here
consider as an ultimate cause,) making a strong
exertion to fulfil the obligation — vehemently re-

sisting any contrary inclination, or resolutely contending against some obstacle;— while the other, though alive to the sense of obligation, makes no effort to act according to that obligation, and yields without resistance to opposing inclinations. This *exertion of free will* in the one, we call *merit ;* the want of it, in the other, *guilt.* The *exertion* so supposed to be employed, from no other cause but the will of the individual in that particular instance, is as different in the idea we form of it, from the general *character* of his mind, as that character is from the *situation* of obligation; or that again, from the beneficial or hurtful *nature of the effect.*

Fitness then is something in the nature of an effect: obligation is a relative situation in which an agent is placed : virtue is a character or quality of his disposition : merit is what accrues to him for the direction and energy of a particular volition. Different degrees of these several qualities of an action may co-exist together in different actions, in like manner as similar figures may exist in different extensions, and similar extensions in different figures.

Having thus, in a general way, separated and characterized the notions severally expressed by the terms *fitness, obligation, virtue* and *merit,* we are now to inquire into the particulars comprehended under each, and to attempt to discover the whole grounds on which each is estimated, whether absolutely or in degree ; and in the course of these inquiries we shall be able to satisfy ourselves that there is nothing whatever apprehended to be fit or obligatory but what reason is capable of perceiving to be so ; that in nothing else do virtue and merit consist, but in the spontaneous disposition, or the wilful choice, to do something which reason is capable of perceiving to be obligatory.

CHAPTER VI.

OF THE DISTINCTIVE NATURE OF THE TRUTHS OF MORAL
SCIENCE.

SECT. I.

Separation of certain Inquiries occasionally confounded.

IF it is the case that certain truths, expressive of moral qualities belonging to actions or agents, are intuitively perceived by reason, the obvious course to be pursued in the farther prosecution of the present inquiry, is, to attempt an enumeration of such truths. Such an enumeration, accordingly, I would now proceed to furnish; but I think it advisable to premise some remarks as to the precise purpose which such an enumeration is calculated, or may be found, to fulfil.

In presenting such a collection of principles as now supposed, stating them, at the same time, to contain the elementary truths of moral science, one may expect to be pressed with such interrogatories as the following: Do these principles then serve to account for all the phenomena of our moral nature? Do they explain, in every case, why we approve of one action and disapprove of another, why we perform this action and avoid performing that one? In fine, do they enable us to tell in what virtue consists; or to form a definition or description of it, comprehending every sort of virtue?

In the view of obviating any embarrassment that might arise from such questions as these, all of which respectively have, on some occasions, been employed as the touchstones by which the soundness and sufficiency of a theory of morals is to be tried, I would first refer to the entirely separate and distinct nature of the two branches of inquiry, into which a theory of morals divides itself. In treating of one of these, the moral theorist is to be considered as exhibiting the doctrines of a particular science; in treating of the other, as exhibiting the philosophy of the human mind, considered in its relation to that science: to that science, namely, as furnishing some of the *objects* about which the faculties and operations of mind are employed. When he states such truths as these — " it is fit that all sentient beings should be happy, rather than miserable"—" the meritorious ought to be happy rather than the guilty" — " whatever is fit to be done, it is obligatory to do" — and the like—he states the primary truths of the science of morals. But how these truths are perceived by our minds, is an inquiry of quite a different description, — belonging, if I may say so, to another branch of science ; and the answer to it is no more to be gathered from these truths themselves, than we can gather from the axioms of Euclid, the nature of those faculties of our mind, by which we judge of mathematical evidence. In like manner, the emotions of approbation and disapprobation are to be explained from the nature of our minds, not from the axioms of morals. If, under the name, then, of the phenomena of our moral nature, sought to be explained, are comprehended the mental acts or operations by which we judge of moral truth, most certainly the axioms which are to be presented do not explain such phenomena ; nor is it any part of their business to do so.

And for these reasons, the question, — do these axioms explain, in every case, why we judge one action good, another bad—is ambiguous; and may be understood as falling under either the one or the other of the two branches of inquiry above distinguished. The answer to be given to it is this : these axioms explain why an action *is* good or bad ; (so far as either term is used to denote a predicate, and not merely a name ;) but they do not explain why *we judge* it so. It is true indeed that we cannot state a proposition as being in itself true, without necessarily implying that we believe it true; and it is in this very way that I have, in the preceding chapters, reasoned from the necessary truth of these axioms, to the peculiar faculty of the mind by which they are perceived. But although the mere enunciation of the axiom involves the affirmation of such belief, it does not explain its nature : that is, it does not assign the situation which this act of belief occupies in a classification of the powers or operation of the mind—which is what is meant by explaining why *we believe it,* considered as a distinct question from why *it is true.* Euclid and the mathematicians teach us that the three angles of a triangle are equal to two right angles ; that parallelograms on the same base, and between the same parallels, are equal, and the like ; and they likewise teach us why this is true ; i. e. they shew how these truths necessarily flow from certain acknowledged first principles of mathematical science. It is left to those who teach the philosophy of the human mind, to shew how or why we believe these truths : that is, to shew how this belief flows from the first principles or general truths of the science of pneumatology—from the general laws of our mental constitution. From peculiar circumstances, however, it has happened that our believing an action to be good has been frequently viewed, not merely as attendant on its being good, but as being really all in which its goodness consists : hence some moral theorists have endeavoured to explain, on one principle, certain phenomena that belong to quite different classes.

An entire neglect of the distinction now insisted upon, and a neglect which occasions much confusion and perplexity, will be found to exist in the systems of several moral theorists: I may instance those of Dr. Adam Smith, and Dr. Thomas Brown. Both these writers, more or less explicitly, in the different parts of their respective works, represent the emotion of the spectator as what really makes the action good or bad: its goodness or badness, according to them, consists in this and in nothing else. Yet both admit, (what it would have been impossible to deny,) that a classification may be made of our various duties; and each indeed furnishes such classification. But the possibility of such classification supposes that there must be some common qualities in good, and in bad actions, respectively, otherwise there could be no general rules of duty —nothing but an enumeration of each and every individual duty: that is, an enumeration of an infinite number of particulars, which is an absurdity: or, if the only common quality in good actions is, that we approve of them, and *vice versa,* the whole of practical morality must be comprehended in this one precept,—Do what is approved. But surely we may desire farther to know, what those actions are that are thus approved: that is, what is the common quality by which such actions are distinguished. Now this question, certainly comprehending a fair and legi-

timate subject of investigation, the two philosophers above named, and I believe others, have
virtually overlooked; or rather have supposed it
to be superseded by an examination of the sentiments of approbation and disapprobation, as felt
by the spectator. Dr. Smith, after stating the
two principal heads of inquiry into which a theory
of morals resolves itself, namely, first, what actions
are good or bad; and, secondly, how do we perceive them to be good or bad,—gives an account
of the different solutions that have been furnished of the first question, in this way:—some
writers, he says, make virtue consist in prudence;
some, in benevolence; some,—among whom the
author ranks himself,—in propriety. Well; wherein, we naturally ask, does the *propriety* of actions
consist? Referring to Dr. Smith's account of propriety, we find that the propriety of any affection
(on which he makes the propriety of the *action* to
depend) consists in its having that quality or degree which a spectator *sympathises* with, i. e. approves of. Is this, in fact, any thing more than
telling us that the common quality of approved actions is simply—that we approve of them?

An inquiry into the manner of our sustenance
by food, might be supposed to be divided into two
heads: what is the nature of those sorts of food,
that are called nutritious? and, by what contrivance in our frame is it, that the nutritious qualities
are rendered subservient to our sustenance? Now

if a person were to state the different opinions that had prevailed in regard to the first question in this manner, — Some persons think that the possession of this chemical ingredient renders food nutritious, others the possession of that ingredient; my opinion is that the nutritive quality of food does not consist in its possessing this or that ingredient, but in the proper mixture of all the different kinds : —suppose a person to propose this statement, and farther to tell us, when asked what a proper mixture was, that it was such a mixture as was found nutritious, — his exposition would be perfectly analogous to that of Dr. Smith.

To explain, then, why a particular action *is good,* is to exhibit the general truth under which this particular one ranges itself, in a *system of morals.* To explain why *we judge* it to be good, is to rank this particular mental act along with the other mental acts of the same class, to which it ought to belong, in *a system of the human mind.*

Referring to the next test which I suppose applied to the principles about to be stated — whether or not they enable us to discover why, in any case, *we perform* a good action rather than a bad one, — I must remark it as a most extraordinary circumstance that this question has ever been taken as equivalent to asking, — wherein consists the moral goodness or badness of an action. Yet several theories of morals have been formed, solely by confounding these two inquiries. The moral obligation of an action constitutes a *motive* for the performance of it ; and therefore it has been somewhat strangely assumed that the converse is true ; and that any motive to which all the different species of good actions might, by any possibility, be traced, may be safely regarded as the cause why we reckon all such actions good. Thus, self love, regard to the will of the Deity, vanity, desire of the esteem and sympathy of others, has, each in its turn, been represented as the prevalent motive of all those actions called good ; and consequently the cause why we perform them, or approve of their performance. Several writers of the highest eminence have, — unaccountably, as it seems to me, — fallen into this confusion of thought.

The first principles of morals, then, will not otherwise explain why *we perform or avoid* any action, than merely as shewing that that action is one that *ought or ought not to be performed.*— But of this more afterwards.

To the question, whether, from the principles to be stated, any definition or description can be given of virtue in general, it is to be replied, that such definition is, in the nature of the thing, an impossibility: the term *virtue* being applied to a variety of qualities, not from any thing that they have in common—the only circumstance on which a definition can be founded—but from certain peculiar relations in which they stand to one another. An action which has the effect of promoting happiness, is fit to be done : whatever is in itself fit, is obligatory on an agent : the regard paid by an agent to the sense of obligation, is the virtue of that agent. So far, *virtue*, in its more strict and proper meaning, is defined. The name however which properly belongs to a quality or character of the agent, is often, in ordinary language, transferred back to that quality of the act, in relation to which we ascribed to him the character in question; that is, we called the agent virtuous, in respect of his performing an obligatory action, we now call the action a virtuous one, because it is the act of a virtuous agent, and one the performance of which made him so. The relation of agent and act gives the same term to the peculiar quality of each. We speak in the same way of an ingenious man, an ingenious machine. The ingenuity of the man, is the quickness, comprehension, and judgment, displayed in contriving the machine : the ingenuity of the machine, is the simplicity and aptitude of the means by which it is made to answer the intended ends. This simplicity and aptitude, being the objects which the ingenuity of the contriver was exerted to produce—we ascribe ingenuity to them. But no one would try to form a definition of *ingenuity*, which would be applicable alike to the mental qualities of the engineer, and to the efficiency of a mechanical engine.

It is to be observed, too, that the terms *obliga-*

tion and *fitness* are expressive of ideas entirely simple, and do not consequently admit of definition. It might be supposed, that, if every action productive of happiness is fit to be done, it would be a correct definition of a fit action, to call it an action productive of happiness; but this is no more the case than it would be a correct definition of an equilateral triangle, to call it a triangle with three equal angles. That it has three equal angles is *true* of an equilateral triangle, but not what expresses our very notion of it — to which the office of a *definition* is confined. So, the fitness of a beneficent action is a truth perceivable in regard to this action; but can by no means be considered as merely expressing what we mean by its possessing such tendency. Obvious as the truth of this remark must appear, it is the neglect of it, the confounding of the benevolent quality of an action with the moral goodness of that quality, as one idea, that has led to one of the most material fallacies connected with the present subject.*

These observations, defining the particular kind of moral truths which, in the dispute regarding the nature of the moral faculty, reason is maintained to discover, will, it is hoped, still farther vindicate the instrumentality of that faculty, by confining such instrumentality within those precise limits beyond which its employment need not be contended for.

* See pages 50 and 122.

SECT. II.

Parallel between Moral and Mathematical Truths.

The views which I entertain as to the source of moral distinctions, naturally lead me to offer an opinion on the question,—whether morality is capable of demonstration, after the manner of mathematics.

If this question meant, whether there are any truths in morals that are necessary and immutable, as opposed to uncertain, contingent, or merely probable, I could of course have no hesitation in answering in the affirmative.

Or, if the question meant, whether there are any of the necessary truths in morals that are the subjects of deduction, as opposed to intuition ; or, which comes to the same purpose, whether we can reason from necessary first principles of morals to other necessary truths, (which is the strict notion of demonstration,)—it seems to me that instances of such demonstration may very easily be shewn. But, in these, the conclusions are so little removed from their premises, that the statement of such demonstrations, like that of some of the elementary theorems of Euclid, seems little better than ingenious trifling.

And therefore, if the question means (as I imagine it ought to be understood) whether we can, by direct reasoning from necessary principles, solve practical difficulties in morals; whether we are indebted to demonstration — to reasoning by progressive steps — for any conclusions in morals which lay hid until such progressive reasoning was employed; whether, in short, morals is a demonstrative science, in the sense that demonstration (in the strict import of the term) ever is, or will be an instrument in ordinary use for ascertaining its truths,— then I can have as little hesitation in saying that morals is not a demonstrative science ; for all ordinary and practical difficulties in morals have reference to matter of *fact*—which, of course, is not subject of demonstration.

But still, the difference between the necessary truths of mathematics, and those of morals, in regard to the application of each to cases of fact, differ only in degree, not in kind.

The moralist tells us that an action which produces fit effects is obligatory. But how, it is asked, are we profited by knowing this, unless we are informed whether any particular action, about which a question may exist, does produce fit effects or not ?

Well, but what more does the mathematician teach us, in regard to any particular point connected with his science ? His information, *so far as it is demonstrative*, is really as hypothetical as that of the moralist. — Suppose there is a triangular field, on each of the sides of which is a four-sided field. The two smaller four-sided fields belong to me, the largest to a neighbour. I wish to exchange with him. Will a mathematician demonstrate that they are equal? Certainly not, any more than the moralist can demonstrate that the effects of any action are fit. He will tell us, —*if* the angle opposite to the largest field is a right angle, and *if* the three four-sided fields are each perfectly square, the field of the one proprietor will be equal to the two fields of the other : and we are left to ascertain, whether, in point of fact, these circumstances exist as supposed or not, just as the moralist leaves us to find out whether the effects of a given mode of conduct will be beneficial or not.

The moralist, then, does not demonstrate that a given action is right or wrong ; but so neither does the mathematician demonstrate that certain fields are equal to one another. The one tells us *if* the action has such and such qualities it is right ; the other, *if* the figures of the fields have such and such qualities, they are equal. In what then does the mathematical differ from the moral truth? It is solely in the degree in which the general hypothetical condition, supporting the particular truth, may be narrowed into a condition of a simpler kind.

The mathematician having found one condition on which a consequence may be established, straightway shews that condition to hold good wherever another exists ; that other, where a third ;

this third, where a fourth ; and this fourth, perhaps, where a fifth exists : and the actual existence of this fifth condition, in any given practical instance, may be very easily ascertained, or much more easily than the first, or even the second, third, or fourth.*

Now the moralist just leaves us at a farther-off stage, whence we have to grope our way with less ease and less certainty.   He carries us, so far as he goes, as securely and as unerringly as the mathematician ; but he leaves us sooner to ourselves.

That the mathematician can push his premises to so much remoter and more specific conclusions than the moralist, arises from the infinite number

---

* Thus, if, in answer to the inquiry about the equality of the fields, the mathematician were merely to tell us, that if my fields were equal to two other fields (which two were equal to my neighbour's,) our possessions would be equal, his information would be of little use to us ; but we can *suppose* that this point might be more easily ascertained than that which we ultimately aim at knowing. If he were to tell us, next, that this condition would hold good, if the space F B C (see Euclid's 47 Prop. 1st Book) were equal to D B A, this might be still more easily found. But if he proceeded, farther, to inform us that this circumstance would depend on the parallelism of the lines B D, L A, F B, G C, and the equality of F B, B D, our task would still be easier.   Lastly, if he said that this equality, and this parallelism, would certainly exist, if angle A were a right angle, and each of the three fields a square ; this would be a point which we should probably be able to ascertain with great ease and certainty.

of *premises* which the former possesses. The principles from which the mathematician reasons are not, as some seem to think, the axioms, but the definitions. (No consequence whatever can be drawn from any, or all, of Euclid's axioms, that would not be as readily admitted as the axiom itself.*) Now every definition of a figure is that of an object more or less complex in the notion we form of it; and the more complex the notion, the more numerous the truths that can be predicated of it. The truths of geometry, again, are expressive only of relation; and thus, the number of figures being infinite, the number of relations infinite, there is no bound to the number of consequences to be drawn from a number of premises without bound. In morals, on the contrary, the

---

* The axiom is nothing but the generalization of a number of particular inferences, perceived to flow from the nature of the figures which are the subjects of the reasoning. It saves the trouble of examining the correctness of each inference of that species, by itself. Yet, perhaps, it is not quite correct to say that the general truth affords no greater conviction than the particular one. It does so, I apprehend, in so far as it presents the subject in the abstract, unincumbered with those generic or specific peculiarities on which the predicate does not depend, and which are apt to distract the attention of the mind, and to obscure or confound the conception, in the peculiar nature of which the truth of the predicate is to be found. And I believe that the mind, previously to giving a full and undoubting assent to any particular truth of the kind supposed, really performs such an abstraction.

principal subjects about which the reasoning is employed, are but few in number, and so simple—(as *happiness* and *misery*)—as not to admit of definition; the number of truths therefore involved in our notion of these subjects must be confined within very narrow limits. Add to which, the truths of morals are not generally truths expressive of *relation*, but of some absolute quality; and absolute qualities, unlike relations, must always be circumscribed in number.

The civil laws of any country may be considered as a body of assumptions, supplying, in morals, the place of that extensive variety of principles from which the mathematician reasons; and, accordingly, we find that trains of demonstrative reasoning may be carried on to any conceivable extent, for the establishment of a legal point, and the whole justice of a case resolved into a hypothetical proposition, where it may be as easy to see whether or not the matter at issue fulfils the condition of the hypothesis, as it is to determine whether a given angle is really a right one, or a given figure a complete square.—Suppose the question to be, whether A or B ought to possess a certain property. By law, then, A has a title, if a certain deed be valid; but this deed is valid if C had the power of executing it; but C had the power of executing it if next heir to D; but C was next heir to D, if D had no lawful children; but D had no lawful children if his marriage was invalid; but his marriage was invalid, if contracted before the dissolution of a former one ; but the former one was undissolved, if the woman was alive at a certain date. Upon this last hypothesis, the whole case is brought to depend ; and it is demonstrated, as strictly as a mathematician can demonstrate a theorem, that, if D's first wife was alive at a supposed time, A is entitled to the property in dispute.

The want of such a body of principles as I here suppose civil laws to supply, must ever prevent morals from being a demonstrative science, in any practical sense of the term. But though not, in this sense, demonstrative,—though its truths, so far as they are necessary truths, are either simply intuitive or but little removed from that,—they possess, on that very account, so much, if possible, greater certainty. In a great many cases, too, the question of fact which a general truth in morals is applied to determine, is as easily brought within the range of that truth, as the question of fact in mathematics is brought within the range of the demonstrated conclusions : so that, if the principle in morals does not advance to meet the practical case, there is as little need of its advancing—the practical case being already sufficiently close to it. That we ought not to inflict gratuitous pain — an intuitive truth, or only two steps of reasoning distant from one—is, to the full, as certain as the conclusion of a mathematical demonstration of any length ; and the question of fact, what does produce gratuitous pain, is, in general, as easily determined, as that, whether an angle of a field is a right one or not.

In both sciences, then, we have universal truths applicable to cases of fact. In the one science, those truths are the results of long processes of reasoning, specific in their nature, and almost infinite in number. In the other science, the universal truths are intuitive, (or nearly so,) general in their nature, and few in number. In both, but principally in the latter, difficulties may occur in the practical application of the general principles : but in mathematics, no more than in morals, will the certainty of the principles either prevent us from assuming wrong data, or from making an erroneous application of principles to those data. If there are disputed or erroneous moral precepts, so there have been disputed or erroneous measurements and calculations.

PART II.

DOCTRINES OF THE SCIENCE OF MORALS.

CHAPTER I.

MORAL AXIOMS, OR FIRST PRINCIPLES OF MORAL TRUTH.

THE following propositions seem to me to possess all the characteristics that are required to constitute *first principles of necessary truth.*—They are true : their truth admits of no proof : it is impossible to conceive that they could ever become untrue, or that the contrary of them could ever be true.

At all events, I should desire it to be considered, whether any defects that may be found in them are inherent in the principle proceeded upon, or only belong to the execution. And, even in regard to defects in execution, I should hope the extreme difficulty of the undertaking will be kept in view : a difficulty, which, even in the case of mathematical axioms and definitions, has not, in every respect, I believe, been satisfactorily overcome.

I. It is fit that every sentient being should be happy, or enjoy pleasure, rather than be miserable or suffer pain.*

II. It is unfit that any sentient being should be miserable or suffer pain.

III. When an agent is under a moral obligation — (when there is something that he ought, something that he ought not to do†) — it is fit that his state should be better‡ if he wills or chooses to fulfil the obligation, than if he does not will or choose to fulfil it; or that his state should be worse§ if he does not will or choose to fulfil the obligation, than if he does will or choose to fulfil it : better in so much greater, worse in so much less a degree, as he exerts the power of free will in a greater or less degree to fulfil the obligation.

---

* Into the distinction between happiness and pleasure, I am not concerned to enter ; nor — to say the truth — am I very well prepared to assign wherein that distinction consists.— For my purpose, they may either be reckoned the same or different.

† *Ought to do* — means, ought to do, or ought to avoid ; *ought not to do*—means, ought not to do, or ought not to omit. The obligation is fulfilled by doing, in the one case, or avoiding in the other ; not fulfilled or violated, by doing, in the one case, by omitting to do in the other.

‡ Or he has *merit*, is of good desert, or deserves well.

§ Or he has *guilt*, is of ill desert, or deserves ill.

DEFINITION.* The power of free will is exerted in a *greater* degree, when exerted to fulfil a small than a great obligation; when exerted with a small than with a great concurring motive; or when exerted against a great than against a small opposing motive.

IV. It is fit that agents equally innocent, meritorious, or guilty, should, respectively, be equally happy or miserable, rather than unequally so.

DEF. Happiness or misery is *more equally divided*, where each person of a number enjoys or suffers the same portion, than where each has only the same chance: more equally where each has the same chance, than where each has not the same chance.

A being who is less happy or more miserable than it is fit he should be, as his desert and situation are compared with the desert and situation of any other being, suffers *injustice*.

V. It is more fit that misery should be removed or relieved, than that happiness should be communicated or augmented.

* This is not properly a definition, but an exemplification of what makes the strength of a volition. But it answers the purpose of a definition.—The same remark applies to other of the definitions.

VI. It is more unfit, or less fit, that misery should be inflicted or increased, than that happiness should not be communicated or increased.

VII. Whatever is, in itself, and in all circumstances, fit or unfit to be, is more fit or unfit to be in a great degree, or to a great extent, than in a small degree or to a small extent.

VIII. An effect which is more fit than unfit, is fit; and *vice versa.**

IX. In proportion as any action is obligatory on an agent, it is fit, or not unfit, that he should be compelled to perform it: and in proportion as it is obligatory on him not to perform any action, it is fit, or not unfit, that he should be prevented from performing it.

X. Whatever effect is, in itself, *fit* to be produced, it is *obligatory* on every agent to act so as it may be produced, — and *vice versa* of unfit effects.

> DEF. The *effect* of an action is only its effect in so far as it takes place in consequence of that action, and would not take place without it.

XI. An obligation which cannot be fulfilled

---

* It may be more fit that a being or several beings, should bear a small evil, than miss a great good: and this even where, in the case of a number, the good may fall to some, the evil to others, yet by equal chances.

without the violation of a greater, is, in respect of it, no obligation.

XII. It is obligatory on every moral agent to discover, to the best of his means, all that is obligatory upon him; and how that which is obligatory may be really, truly, and actually performed.

> DEF. *Virtue* is the spontaneous inclination to fulfil moral obligation.
>
> DEF. *Depravity* is indifference about the fulfilment of moral obligation, or the spontaneous aversion to fulfil it.

XIII. Whatever it is obligatory on an agent to do, or not obligatory upon him not to do, and in the same proportion, he has a *right* to do, and no one has a right that it should not be done.

XIV. That which it is obligatory on any agent to do to another, that other has a right to have done.

XV. Whatever it is obligatory on an agent not to do, and in the same proportion, he has no right to do, and no one has a right that it should be done.

XVI. Whatever it is obligatory on any agent not to do to another, that other has a right not to have done.

> DEF. The doing to any being what he has a right should not be done, or the not doing what he has a right should be done, is an *injury*.

XVII.   When an agent has committed an injury, it is obligatory upon him to make reparation or compensation to the person injured, as well for the injury, as for the evil in the infliction of which the injury consisted.

———

Though the following propositions on the nature of happiness and misery appear to me necessary truths, they are not properly first principles of *morals*.   But in the demonstration of many practical duties, they must, at all events, be advanced as postulates. — That a being ought to be happy rather than miserable, is a universal truth.   If it is the *fact* that he is made unhappy in being deceived, it follows that he ought not to be deceived; and this, alike, whether his aversion to being deceived is necessary or implanted.

XVIII. Every being must be so far happier as he obtains what he desires or wishes, so far more miserable as he does not obtain what he desires or wishes.

XIX. Every being must desire to know the truth, and be averse to being deceived.

XX. Every being must desire to be loved, approved, and regarded by other beings; and be averse to be hated, disapproved, or despised by them.

XXI. Every being must be so far happier as

he expects happiness or pleasure, so far more miserable as he expects misery or pain.

XXII. Every being must suffer pain or uneasiness in being prevented from doing what he would will or choose to do.

XXIII. Every being must suffer pain or uneasiness in being deprived of any means of enjoyment of which he is in possession, or in expectation.

XXIV. Every being must find pleasure in the consciousness and contemplation of virtue, and *vice versa*.

XXV. Every being must experience pain and uneasiness in being *injured*, or treated *unjustly*.

———

From the axioms and definitions may be formed certain theorems or demonstrations, which are also universal truths in morals : thus —

It is more fit that happiness should be promoted than misery. But whatever it is fit should be, it is fit should be in a great degree, or to a great extent, rather than in a small degree, or to a small extent. Therefore it is fit that a being should be made happy in a great, rather than in a small degree ; that many should be made happy rather than a few, &c.

It is fit that happiness should be equally, rather than unequally divided. But whatever is fit to be in itself, is fit to be in a great degree, &c. Therefore it is fit that happiness should be more, rather than less, equally divided. But, by definition, happiness is more equally divided, when each of a number has an equal share, than when each has only an equal chance. Therefore it is more fit that happiness should be divided in equal shares to each, than only by equal chances.

These are offered merely as instances of strict demonstration occurring in morals ;* and to shew that certain propositions which might otherwise be thought first principles, are really not such, but deductions from principles. As demonstrations, they must, — for reasons already assigned, — appear *trifling*.

For the proper use and application of the axioms now stated, two remarks require to be offered ; both of which, as relating to a very abstract subject, can scarcely be expressed but in technical terms ; but will yet admit of plain enough illustration.

First. What is, in every axiom, predicated of a certain subject, being involved in the conception we form of that subject, must be a necessary truth, and therefore general, and holding good under every circumstance. It only holds good however ih relation to that subject, and so far only as that subject is concerned ; and not in regard to any

* See also *note* in page 217.

other subject with which that one may be mixed or connected.

For instance; we say, it is fit that happiness should be promoted rather than misery: but again, that a guilty agent should be in a worse state than otherwise, on account of his guilt: that is, taking the notion of *happiness*, and of a *living being* in the abstract, and without regard to any other consideration, it is, so far, or in this single respect, — whatever it may be in others, —*fit* that he should enjoy happiness rather than suffer misery. To another consideration, namely, that of his *guilt*, another predicate applies; and in any case of this sort, the first axiom must fail in its application, not because it does not still remain equally true, and *so far* applicable, but because another is as true, and more applicable.

The effect of the remark now made is just to this purpose, that we must understand every axiom as having some such qualification as one of these attached to it — "so far, and excluding all other circumstances but what are stated," — "abstractedly from all other considerations," — "all other things being alike."

Secondly. The subject of a predicate may be what we have not been able to acquire a notion of, until this very predicate has itself been made the subject of another predicate; nor does this involve circular reasoning. It is fit that an agent who wills to perform his duty, should be rewarded.

Here, a proposition, asserting some thing to be fit, supposes the notion of *obligation* or *duty :* but the notion of obligation itself supposes the previous one of fitness. The matter proceeds in this course :—The promotion of happiness is fit. What is thus fit in itself, is obligatory on a moral agent. If one moral agent wills to do what is thus fit, another wills to do the contrary, it is *fit*, again, that the first should be rewarded, the second punished. Other illustrations of this sort of *sequence* will be found in the course of this work : but all proceeding from a perception that something is fit, originally, of itself, and on its own account.

———

It has now been found that the general affirmation made regarding any action, that it is *good*, or the contrary, may contain, or stand for a variety of propositions; some of which are propositions, or *truths*, in the strict meaning — *asserting* something ; others, only *definitions — naming* something. In an inquiry into the mode in which such propositions or truths are discovered, I have ascribed such discovery to the faculty of reason; and, finally, have attempted an enumeration of these truths, as not only containing the first principles of moral science, but as thence forming the source of all our other moral notions, the names of which I have also attempted to define. It will now fall

to be inquired, how far these principles and definitions are just, and answer the purpose they are
intended to serve : namely, to explain in general
what actions are *good* or *bad*, in all the senses in
which this may be affirmed.   The inquiry will fall
to be conducted both according to an analytic and
a synthetic method : that is, it will be attempted
to be shewn, that to whatever actions or agents the
common judgments or feelings of mankind apply
any moral quality or distinction, such quality or
distinction is reducible, in the mode of its application, to some or other of the attributes above specified, under the names of fitness, obligation, virtue or depravity, merit or guilt; and that the degree in which any action or character is conceived
to possess any of these attributes, will correspond
with the principles and definitions above stated :
and also, on the other hand, that, from these principles and definitions, again, may be deduced, by
direct reasoning, the ordinary doctrines of practical morality, and the rules according to which
virtue and vice, merit and guilt, are estimated.
Between these two modes of illustration, however,
it is not proposed to maintain a regular separation ;
but to employ both promiscuously, as occasion
may suggest.

   It is proper also to add, that though I conceive
all the foregoing axioms to be truths perceived by
reason, their claim to be received as *first principles of moral science* does not at all depend upon

the validity of this or any other hypothesis as to the faculty by which they are discovered. Even if approbation and disapprobation are mere *feelings* — yet if these axioms are the most general expressions to which those feelings can be reduced, they are entitled to be considered as first principles of morals. All the difference is, that one person would say — reason perceives that happiness ought, misery ought not to be promoted; another — the promotion of happiness is viewed with a pleasing, of misery with a painful emotion. In the inquiries then that are now to be followed, we meet on common ground. By whatever faculty we distinguish right and wrong, there is still a question *what* that faculty perceives to be right, and *what* it perceives to be wrong. Upon this question, and upon what others may rise out of it, we who maintain, and you who deny the instrumentality of reason in our moral determinations, may, indifferently, either split or agree, without any regard to what may be our respective opinions upon that head.

CHAP. II.

OF THE MORAL FITNESS OF CERTAIN ENDS OR EFFECTS.

LITTLE requires to be said upon this subject, as the axioms relating to *fitness* convey all that can well be stated, and illustrations without number will at once suggest themselves.

It will perhaps occur that if it is morally fit that there should be happiness rather than misery, much rather than little happiness, that many should be happy rather than few, then, as no number of happy beings, no degree of happiness, can be imagined, but what would admit of increase, it would become morally fit that there should be an infinite number of beings infinitely happy—which is absurd. Now of these two propositions—on the one hand, that the number of living beings and the degree of their happiness must each have finite bounds; on the other, that their number and the degree of their happiness *ought* always to be great rather than small — of these two propositions, all that we can say is, that we can see where they would cross one another,

but we cannot give up either.   And I apprehend
it cannot be so properly said that they contradict
or falsify, as that, at some point, they necessarily
touch and bound one another.

It is a question that has always presented itself
to the philosophical inquirer, how infinite power,
guided by infinite wisdom, and prompted by infinite
benevolence, could have suffered the existence of
that host of moral and physical evils that afflict our
earthly condition.

The question is not more natural to be asked, than
difficult to be answered.   Yet it would seem, if I
mistake not, that the difficulty or even impossibility
of solving this problem has induced few or none to
suppose a limitation of the divine attributes. There
seems, so to speak, to be an answer to the difficulty lying somewhere in the recesses of the human
breast, though we cannot drag it into light.   We
cannot persuade ourselves that there is either a
want of power, a want of wisdom, or a want of goodness, in the Being who formed us, and the universe
in which we dwell.   But in whatever way we may
strive to approximate the solution — whether we
try to satisfy ourselves with the reflection that in
whatever position of comfort and happiness the
living creation might have been placed, a greater
extension, a greater degree of comfort and happiness would still have been possible *ad infinitum*,
so that the same difficulty, why were not things
better ordered, must have existed under any cir-

cumstances ;—whether we suppose that there are bounds to possibility undiscoverable by us, which (as the supposition would involve a contradiction) even omnipotence itself cannot pass ;—or whether we suppose that the Deity has voluntarily and purposely confined himself within a limited circle of means, a definite range of possibilities, in order to manifest his power and wisdom to his creatures ; (for how, it might be asked, could wisdom appear in contriving means, where the end was to be attained without means? how could power be shewn where no opposing tendencies or obstacles were permitted to exist?) — or whether we suppose that, as regards the case of a created being, an experience of evil is necessary for an otherwise unattainable relish for future good ; that happiness which is not increasing, ceases to be happiness ; or that victory over trials and difficulties, in the exercise of free agency, is necessary to the perfection of a species of moral excellence, and felicity springing from it, not otherwise to be acquired ; or that the perfect justice of the Deity cannot dispense happiness to those who have not deserved it by patience, fortitude, diligence, superiority to temptations, (all supposing the existence of evil,)—whatever of these solutions we adopt, whether we adopt them all, or a part of them, or adopt others, we shall never adopt the supposition that it could have seemed to the Deity *morally right* to inflict pain *simply for the sake of doing so:* more easily than we could suppose this, indeed, we could suppose the Deity but imperfectly bent on doing what was morally fit, imperfectly able to contrive, or imperfectly able to fulfil. The existence of the question, then, why was pain or evil permitted, fortifies the truth of the proposition, that happiness is essentially fit, misery unfit; the difficulty or impossibility of answering the question does not affect the truth of that proposition. We can perhaps suppose that happiness might be so excessive as to become uneasiness; we unavoidably perceive that the degree and extent of happiness must be finite; but this can never cease to appear morally fit, that happiness should *be*, rather than misery; happiness great, rather than small in degree; happiness widely, rather than narrowly distributed. This much at least is certain and indisputable, that whatever might be the divine purpose in permitting or occasioning the existence of evil, there is no principle in our intellectual or moral constitution that teaches us, in any case, that evil *as* evil, and for the sake of its being evil, *ought* by us to be permitted or occasioned — no principle which, if it teaches any thing, does not teach the contrary. So far as our reason or our conscience informs us, so far as we can penetrate into the intentions of God and nature, so far as the will of God has been explicitly revealed to us, there is, in every case, a *moral fitness* in the promotion of happiness, as such, — in the prevention or removal of misery, as such. To human agents at least, these must always be ends; ends which, with human means, can never be pursued to excess. Even if there may be other ends besides these, and by which these may occasionally be interfered with or superseded, these can never cease to be ends; even if there be cases in which pain ought to be inflicted or happiness withheld, it cannot be for the sake of inflicting pain, for the sake of withholding happiness. That happiness, simply as such, ought to be promoted rather than misery, that happiness should, simply as happiness, be promoted in a great degree, to a great extent, rather than in a small degree or to a small extent — these are propositions which must of necessity be received as at least *among* the first principles of morals, under every system, every theory which man can possibly form.

The question has sometimes been put, whether the promotion of virtue is not in itself something fit, as distinct from the promotion of happiness? But the promotion of virtue must always be the promotion of happiness; since virtue, both as a subject of contemplation and a source of conduct, necessarily produces happiness. To put such a question then is really to ask whether the promotion of virtue is not fit, as distinct from that from which it yet can never be made distinct.

This much, at all events, seems certain, that the perception that the promotion of happiness is fit, must necessarily precede the perception that the promotion of virtue is fit; because without the former perception, we could not so much as form a notion of what virtue is; and the subsequent perception that the promotion of virtue is itself fit, is another instance of that sort of reproductive sequence in our moral sentiments that has already been observed.

CHAPTER III.

OF OBLIGATION OR DUTY AS LYING UPON AN AGENT.

SECT. I.

Of general *Obligations, as arising from the proper and immediate Effects of Actions.*

IN the last chapter, I treated of the *fitness* of actions, or of that quality which belongs to the *end, result,* or *effect* of an action, without reference either to any *duty,* conceived as lying upon an *agent,* or to any approvable or rewardable conduct in such agent. That a living being should be happy rather than miserable, does not merely mean, that it is the duty of a moral agent to render him happy, or that this is what a moral agent would be praised or rewarded for. The first proposition is true, absolutely, and in itself, and presupposed in those that follow. Immediately connected with the notion of fitness, however, and arising out of it, is that of *obligation or duty,* which the mind at once forms on conceiving of some fit or unfit *effect,* as what a moral *agent* may produce.

Our notion of the obligation of any action is

just that of the amount of cause or reason why that action *should* be performed. Now that an action produces a fit effect, is certainly a cause or reason for the performance of it ; that it produces a fitter effect, is a greater reason ; that it produces a less fit effect, is a less reason. We immediately and necessarily perceive then, that if any effect is, in itself, fit to be produced, it is obligatory on an agent to produce it, and *vice versa ;* and that, in proportion as the effect of an action is more or less fit, such action is more or less obligatory.

The various deductions applicable to the circumstances of mankind, that may be drawn from the principle now stated, — directing what particular actions are to be performed, what avoided, fixing the comparative obligation of different sorts of actions, or determining what line of conduct is proper in various supposed cases, — constitute the *practical rules of morality;* and I am now to exhibit the manner in which these rules are formed.

It must be specially kept in view, that the subject of present inquiry is not, what sort of conduct makes an agent a *virtuous* agent, or what confers *merit* upon him. It has just been observed, that our notion of an *end's* being a fit end, is not equivalent with that of its being the duty of an agent to produce it ; but that, on the contrary, an obligation to pursue the end, presupposes that some ends are, *in themselves*, fit to be pursued. In like manner to shew that actions are obligatory on an agent, is very different indeed from shewing what would be virtuous or meritorious in that agent. The virtue or merit of the agent, that is, the disposition or endeavour of such agent to do his duty, presupposes that something is his duty, and his duty independently of what may be his disposition or endeavour.

Still less, if possible, must we, when pointing out what makes certain actions morally obligatory, be viewed as explaining what generally makes men perform such actions. Men perform good actions from many principles besides a perception of moral obligation ; and what we are to investigate is only why men *ought* to perform certain actions, independently of any impulses which they may feel from natural instincts, passions, or affections.

The just way of arriving at a knowledge of the foundations of moral duty, is to suppose a being destitute of all the natural instincts, affections, and passions, which lead to the preservation of the individual and the species — still, however, supposing him to be possessed of different sources of happiness and misery — for without these, as formerly shewn, no moral notions could possibly come to exist. Though a man were destitute of parental affection, there would still be *a reason why he ought* to nourish and protect his children ; this would be *morally right* rather than the contrary. Though he were destitute of the desire of food, and derived no pleasure from taking nourishment, it would still be morally right that he should take nourishment. So, though he felt no instinctive resentment against injuries, no gratitude for favours (if this were possible,) it would still be morally right that he should punish the one, reward the other. Now *why* such things are thus morally right, is all our present question. The fact that man possesses certain instincts and affections, is a fact which (as I shall have occasion to shew) affects the principles in which moral rules are formed : so, from the fact that he has such instincts and affections, there may sometimes be shewn a moral propriety in his allowing these instincts and affections a general influence on his conduct. But this *fact* is yet altogether different from the *truth* that he *ought* to perform certain actions ; and this truth is one which has grounds of its own perfectly independent of that fact.

In a great, perhaps in by much the greater number of cases, the application of the general principle above given is attended with no difficulty. By simply conjoining this principle with those particular moral axioms that determine what ends are morally fit or unfit, and in what relative degree, we obtain certain rules of morality that almost suffice for the direction of conduct in every instance. The first and most imperious rule of morality is, — do no harm or hurt; occasion no misery, pain or uneasiness ; — the second — prevent or relieve, as far as possible, all misery, pain or uneasiness ;—the third—create as much as possible of positive happiness, pleasure, and satisfaction. — Promote the happiness, prevent or relieve the misery, rather of the deserving, than of the undeserving. In general, promote happiness, relieve misery, rather equally than unequally—avoid doing evil to one for the sake of doing good to another. These are rules that invariably hold good ; rules which any one who seeks sincerely to apply, cannot often fail in the performance of his duty.*

In certain cases, however, the application of the general principles now stated is attended with considerable difficulty, arising principally from one or other of the following sources :

First. An action, harmless or beneficial in its direct or immediate effects, may be hurtful in its collateral or remote effects, and *vice versa.*

Secondly. An action which, performed by one agent, has no effect at all, or a beneficial effect, may, when performed by a number of agents, have a pernicious effect, and *vice versa.*

Thirdly. A rule of conduct, which, when understood and applied in its strict and just meaning, would be of harmless or beneficial tendency, may yet be such that the ignorance, self-deceit, or perversity of human agents would, in fact, explain and apply it so as to make it of pernicious tendency.

* These rules are the conclusions of so many syllogisms, the major proposition of each of which is the 10th Axiom, the minor, the 2d, 5th, 1st, 3d, 4th, 6th — respectively.

As the difficulty in the first of these cases is more of a practical than of a theoretical kind, it does not seem at present to call for illustration; and I accordingly proceed to explain the theory of moral rules, in regard to the second and third cases.

When we say a man may, or ought to perform such and such an action, or such action is the duty of a man, or that of which the performance is allowable or obligatory, the subject of every such proposition is necessarily a general term, and the proposition a general proposition. If we say that a man may tell an untruth, we say that any man may tell an untruth, or any untruth. If we say that, under any particular circumstances described, a man may tell an untruth, we say that in every case where the circumstances are such as described, a man, and every man in such circumstances, may tell an untruth. If we say that a man and woman may have sexual intercourse, we say that any or every man and woman may have intercourse. If we say that a man and woman particularly circumstanced may have intercourse, we say that every man and woman so circumstanced may have intercourse,—and all this just as in saying that a triangle contains two right angles, we say that every triangle contains two right angles. Each of the terms, *man, woman, untruth,* as necessarily represent a *species* in the one case, as *triangle* does in the other.

And not only this, but if we pronounce concerning any particular action, under all the peculiar circumstances with which it may be described, or beheld to be accompanied—this is an allowable or right action, or, this is a bad action—we cannot be taken to pronounce only that this individual action is allowable or wrong, (as the case may be,) or even that all actions which resemble this one in all its minute particulars are of the character supposed. The circumstances which do not appear to influence the obligation to perform or avoid the action, are separated, in the minds of those who hear the proposition, from the circumstances that do; and the action to which our proposition relates is taken as the representative of every action resembling it in those essential points.

But even when immaterial peculiarities are abstracted, it may appear that the judgment given in regard to the propriety or impropriety of the action, though that judgment may have been influenced by each of the remaining particulars, did not wholly depend upon all of them together. After one circumstance is abstracted, the same proposition may appear applicable to the action, but in a greater or less degree, and so after another and a third are abstracted.

As in speaking of an action then, we speak not merely of an individual, but of a species, a class, or even a genus, — what we affirm of that action will only be true (true as we *shall be understood —*

and no proposition is true but that which is true as it is understood) so far as it holds true of the species, class, or genus ; and in proportion as we fail of limiting our judgment, as expressed, to the specific or generic peculiarities, that judgment may be, as understood, a false one.

If then an action is obligatory or the contrary as its effects are fit or unfit, and if an action always means a species or class of actions — the effect of an action is the effect of a species or class of actions, and the effect of a species or class is that from which we compute the obligation of the action.

In many cases, a reference to the *species* of an action does not alter the judgment we should form regarding it as an *individual*. In other cases, the obligation is materially affected, sometimes wholly created by such a reference.

I. The obligation of an action arises solely in reference to its *species*, in those cases where an effect is produced only by the *combination* of a variety or multitude of actions.

Most of the offices performed in the formation, advancement, ordinary conduct, and defence of political communities, and in the promotion of works and establishments of public utility, are of this description. Individual acts cannot, in such cases, be otherwise obligatory, than as representing the whole *class* by which the effect is produced.

And, from the very nature of those cases in which concert or combination is required, it must necessarily be the first and most essential duty of an agent to promote such concert, whether to the best effect or not. A man must not here, as in other cases afterwards to be described, say, in reference to his own convictions of the most expedient course, this is *my duty*, and I must follow it without regard to consequences, — for it is only in regard to consequences that his duty, in such cases, is at all determined. Most of the evils which communities usually encounter in forming or altering plans of civil government, arise from the want of concert, and of that spirit of *compromise* which is essential to concert.*

Under the notion of an *effect* produced only by a combination of actions, is the *ease and confidence* which we enjoy, when a certain obligation is ordinarily fulfilled among mankind, and the terror and anxiety we should suffer, if the same obligation were frequently violated.

Remove the obligation to charity and benevolence, and the evil which would consist in the ac-

---

* Questions of expediency, however, are so often mixed up with questions of *right* in such cases, that an aversion to compromise may be the reverse of blameable. But even where *rights* are concerned, if each party believes the other conscientious, there is the same reason for compromise, as in regard to mere expediency : — at all events, the question is not merely what is best, or most just, but what is most practicable.

tual distress that might remain unrelieved, would be little to that which would consist in the apprehension felt by those who might have cause to look forward to the enduring of such distress. Loosen the bands of truth and honesty, and the real loss we might suffer from fraud, peculation, or treachery, would be little to the uneasiness we should experience in the thought that no reliance could be placed in the integrity or fidelity of those around us.

Strange as it may appear, the actual evil produced by an individual crime of a species which is deservedly looked upon as pre-eminently atrocious, namely, that of murder, is often so little, (if any at all,) as scarcely to admit of being calculated. — Viewing the loss of life as an affair of judgment and rational estimation, and setting the instinctive horror of death out of the question, I believe many men might very fairly doubt, to say no more, whether a continuance of worldly existence was, on the whole, to be desired; whether, setting the tedium and positive evils of life against its ease and its enjoyments, a state of insensibility would not really be preferable.*—What then, if I am un-

* I speak here without reference to the consideration of a *future state;* because the rules of morality, as affecting the taking away of life, are formed without respect to such consideration, and upon the instinctive and habitual feeling that death is an *evil.* Looking to the existence of a future state of retribution, to take away the life of a good man, is to confer on him the most invaluable favour.

awares shot through the head ? — I lose what is of little value, — lose, in an instantaneous and easy manner, what, if left to the course of natural decay or disease, would probably be withdrawn amid prolonged and exquisite agonies. — But then, on the other hand, what comparison would even these agonies bear with the state of anxious terror and horrid alarm in which the whole of every man's life would be passed, did murder cease to be a crime, and were the arm of the assassin, either in reality or imagination, to be continually stretched over us!

II. As the total effect resulting from any species of action must frequently depend upon the number of particular actions of which it consists, the obligation of that species of action must be affected accordingly. — To understand what is meant by the number of actions in a species, it must be observed that an action which can be reckoned *obligatory,** can be only a *hypothetical* action : one of which an agent contemplates the performance, without its being certain either that he will or will

* In general throughout the chapter, or where the idea is not specially expressed otherwise, an *obligation*, or an obligation to *perform*, stands either for an obligation to do, or for an obligation to avoid doing something. Obligation, in its very meaning, can never refer to merely *passive* conduct, — even where it is obligation to *omit* or *abstain*. The agent is only *passive* in the same sense as a man is passive, who keeps immoveable in a position from which a force is applied to remove him. His very passiveness is exertion.

not perform it.   When we tell a man that he *ought* to do something, that it is his duty, or obligatory upon him to do so, we necessarily understand these two things : First, That it is not what he is inclined, or ready, or at least certain to do, independently of its being shewn to be a point of duty ; and, secondly, that its being shewn to be a point of duty, creates a motive, more or less powerful, to the observance of it; that the visible existence of a great obligation is a stronger motive than that of a small obligation, and *vice versa*.   It would evidently be quite idle to say to a man, — this is your duty, — were it either what he would do although not his duty,* or would not the rather do, although it were ; or although it were so in a great, rather than in a small degree.

The actions of any species or class then, which we can pronounce to be obligatory, are all the *hypothetical* actions of that species or class ; and the number of which the class consists, must be according to the number of agents who can perform the action, and of the opportunities and inducements to perform it.   Hence these circumstances affect the obligation.

Assassination by poison, or where the victim is under the dominion of sleep, or otherwise in a helpless condition, is reckoned a more dangerous

---

* It cannot be said to be his duty if he is certain to do it.— May he then not do it ? nay — but this very question makes his doing of it *hypothetical* — on which ensues the obligation.

crime than open murder by violence. Every one has it in his power to commit the first; comparatively few the second.

Stealing of cattle and other unprotected property, theft by a servant in the house of his master, are generally punished with more severity than other species of depredation which present fewer opportunities and facilities.

Vices of impurity require to be curbed by a stronger sense of obligation, both on account of the power and universality of the impulse which leads to the practice of them, and because of the almost unlimited number of means and opportunities of gratification. Some species too, on account of such causes more peculiarly affecting them, require to be guarded in even a much greater degree than others. Thus, crimes of incest. If no greater moral turpitude were attached to the illicit connexion of the sexes among near relatives, and such as usually live together, than among parties comparatively strangers,* a greater amount of profligacy, from the increased number of occasions, would ensue in the one case than in the other.

But it is only when an action is viewed as

---

* If a natural repugnance exists, it does not alter the case. The consideration stated may be presumed to be the *final cause* why such repugnance was implanted :—at all events, our only inquiry here is as to the grounds of *moral obligation*, independently of natural repugnance.

the *representative of a species*, that the degree
of opportunity or temptation to commit such action, can seem at all to affect the obligation to
avoid the commission.   In such cases a man may
just occasion as much harm by committing one
crime* as another — *if he actually commits the one
or the other*.   But the one may be of a kind which
it is ten to one that any given *individual* either
cannot commit, or may be little inclined to commit; the other may be of a description that every
one both can and would commit.   Under no obligation, then, or under equal degrees of it, we
should have ten times as much evil done in the
one case as in the other.

It is to be recollected however that, speaking
with reference to the case of a perfect moral
agent, there is no such thing as *degree* in obligation.   If I am under an obligation to perform any
action, I am under an obligation entirely and actually to do it: if under an obligation at all, I
cannot be less; I cannot, in any other case, be
more.   But when it is certain, as with respect to
human agents it is, that obligation will not be
actually and perfectly fulfilled, while yet a persuasion of its existence will have some degree of

* Illustrations of the theory of moral rules, are more easily
found among *wrong* than among *right* actions — the obligation
to avoid crimes requiring, for obvious reasons, to be more accurately proportioned and defined, than that to perform actions
positively good.

influence, it becomes necessary that the obligation, in the apprehension of the agent, should be proportioned to the occasion that exists for its influence ; greater, as the effect is more fit, and as there is less inducement otherwise, and independently of moral obligation, for the agent to act in conformity with such obligation,— and *vice versa.*

The considerations now offered explain, in part, the nature of those duties which are called *duties of honour*, or those which a man is under no external constraint to perform. These are commonly said to be more obligatory than other duties : but if we look to the real nature of the case, it will appear, not that these are, properly speaking, more obligatory, but that the others with which they are compared, are such as do not admit of this attribute at all. If I have received money without granting a receipt, I am bound in honour not to deny it. But am I not under a similar obligation not to deny that for which I have granted a receipt ? no more than I am under an obligation not to pull the sun out of the firmament ; — and for the same reason — because it is out of my power. In this way the one action is more obligatory than the other, for much the same reason that a bullet is heavier than a smell or a sound.

III. In like manner as, when a beneficial effect is only the result of a combination of actions, the obligation of an action is increased — sometimes indeed entirely created — by its being viewed as the representative of its species (i. e. of all those actions by the combination of which the effect is produced) — so, when a particular effect can be produced by one action, and does not admit of increase by repetition of the action, a reference to the species of that action *diminishes* the obligation.

If any one of a great number of persons may perform a particular beneficial action, an obligation on one (being necessarily expressed by a general proposition) is an obligation on every one. But the *effect* of an action, in reference to which it is obligatory, is, (by the definition,) that which would be produced by the action, and would not be produced without it. The chance then, that, in the case supposed, any one action would produce an effect that would not be produced without it (an *absolute* obligation to produce it lying on each of the whole number) is smaller as the number is greater; consequently the relative obligation (relative as between this action and another of a less numerous species) becomes diminished.*

When it is absolutely certain that an action will be performed by some one or other out of a number, independently of moral obligation, no obligation exists on any of them; because the

* A practical error in such cases is to suppose even the *absolute* obligation extinguished. Hence the proverb " Every body's business is no body's business."

action would produce no *effect*, i. e. no effect that would not be produced without it.

The consideration, now illustrated, that the *effect* of an action in morals must frequently be taken to mean the effect of that *species* of action, explains why we are often morally obliged to perform an action which (individually) does no good, or abstain from one which (individually) does no harm. To say that the species is obligatory, is to say that every individual of it is so; but, as we have seen, an individual action of an obligatory species is often entirely without effect.

But when the necessity of making an action obligatory arises only from the impossibility of distinguishing it from a *class* that must be so, that necessity must appear to fail wherever a *speciality* exists which may serve as a distinction—more particularly if an advantage would (as it often might) arise from excepting the *special* case.

To meet this consideration, it is to be observed, first, that it is of the very nature of a speciality of the kind we are speaking of, that it must belong to no greater number of cases than what may be excepted from the rule without losing the main object for which the rule provides. (We assume that the loss of the rule, would be greater than the loss of all the exceptions.) A *difference* from other cases does not constitute a *speciality*, or every case might be a special case, — which is absurd.

A speciality must be a difference which, *more than any other difference,* is a fit subject of exception. The same remark holds in excepting species from classes, as in excepting individuals from species.

A familiar instance of delusion in this respect occurs in the mode in which men are often led to dispense with the rules of personal and domestic economy. Some particular piece of outlay appears to have its particular justification; another of the same kind has its particular justification also;—so a third—a fourth. Every case in which we are disposed to incur this sort of outlay is a *particular* case,— in other words, no case is so. Still, this *species* of expense is altogether, and as a species, distinguished from every other species. Whether it is hospitality, or books, or paintings, or field-sports, or furniture, or dress, or living, it is that in regard to which we chance to have a peculiar taste — a peculiar knowledge,— to lie under a peculiar habit — a peculiar necessity ; — an unrestrained indulgence of this *species* of expense cannot much interfere with our economical plans. Thus, from excepting an individual, we come to except a species. By and by, some other expense of a different species is found to be indispensable —a second,—a third,—a fourth,—each on some *particular* ground which distinguishes it from every other of its species, — till at length the whole species becomes *another particular species.* Thus every one occasion of superfluous outlay is found to differ from every other occasion, every species from every other species; until at last it comes to be found that every superfluous expense whatever has its peculiar justification — that is, that no one has it above another; and that retrenchment must take place in every particular, or not at all.

Allowing however a speciality to be real, there is one very large class of actions, — and that class in regard to which it is that occasional departures from the general rule would seem to be most advantageously practised, — where yet no special exceptions can be admitted, without frustrating the very ends for which such exceptions would be made. I allude to *acts of deceit* — under which is here included, not merely deceptive *communication*, express, or implied, but every species of act into which deceit necessarily enters—deceptive offences against the property, the person, or the feelings. It is plain that if you specify any particular case in which deceit would be allowable, no man would *trust* another in such a case, and therefore would not be deceived,—so that of course the purpose of the deceit would remain unanswered; or, on the other hand, if the deceit could not be guarded against, the party exposed to it would incur all the pains that arise from the consciousness or suspicion of deceit. If it were made allowable to tell a man that his friend or relative is alive, while he is really dead, no man would ever believe such a thing, even when the information might be true. If there is **any case** in which it is made allowable to cheat me of my money, I will trust no one in such a case; if I cannot avoid trusting, I shall necessarily suffer the uneasiness of supposing that I am cheated. From the very nature of the case, then, it is scarcely, if at all, possible to imagine any circumstance in which deceit can be morally right.

But, in the next place, even where specialities, strictly so called, do exist, and when an accommodation to them would not merely do no harm, but on the contrary do good; nay, when actual harm would be produced by the want of such accommodation, — we must often neglect such specialities, and follow the general rule; and this notwithstanding that the object gained by the rule would not, in any degree or manner whatever, be frustrated by its being subjected to the exception.

Two causes prevent men from judging correctly of right and wrong, — ignorance, and self-love. From the first, they often do wrong when acting to the best of their unbiassed judgment with the intention of doing right ; from the second, when present passion or habitual selfishness represents that as right, which, if coolly observed in another person, they would not hesitate to pronounce as wrong. It is not enough then that a speciality be such *in fact*. It must admit of being at once so clearly defined, and so easily understood, that there may be no risk of its being attached to

cases not really possessing it ; otherwise, to admit
the speciality, would be to give up the rule.
Setting aside the danger of ignorance or delusion,
it is often necessary to deprive good men of a discretion which they might only misuse accidentally
or involuntarily, if we would restrain bad men
from wilful abuse : it being more easy to convict
a man of a slight departure from a prescribed rule,
than of even a flagrant abuse of a discretionary
power.

Those whose business it is to make laws either
for communities, or for the particular branches of
service required by such communities, such as the
judicial, military and revenue departments, come
to be very fully aware of the necessity of enjoin-
ing the universal application of certain specific
rules : and whoever will observe the progress of
moral systems, and of legislation, whether general
or particular, (which is a branch of morals,) will
perceive that the progress of all rules formed for
the direction of human conduct, is, as regards the
nature of such rules, from general to specific ; and
as regards their application, from discretionary to
specific, from specific to universal. — A revenue
officer is authorised to relieve from their burdens,
those whose situations from poverty or otherwise,
are *peculiar*. He soon finds the situation of all
his intimate friends, near neighbours, acquaint-
ances, to be thus peculiar ; the consequence comes
to be that the burden is allotted by chance, or

what, in regard to the justice of the allotment, is worse than chance. The first remedy is to bind him to specific cases; but the narrower, like the wider boundary, is also overleaped. The last step is to cut off the dispensing power altogether; the necessary consequence of which is the constant application of the same rule to a variety of cases differing much from one another; and in regard to some of which it is productive, it may be, of flagrant injustice.

That the nature and operation of general rules may be more fully understood, we must keep in view that to whomsoever a rule of conduct is given, such person and no other has the explanation and application of that rule. It can only take effect as he understands it, and in the cases in which he perceives it to apply. This point is of the utmost consequence to be attended to, since it contains the principle on which hangs the great difference between the general or theoretical, and the specific or practical rules of morality.

If a man is directed to act justly, we necessarily leave him to determine what *is* acting justly. If we give him specific rules, such as to keep his lawful promises, not to violate another's property, or the like, we must, in a similar manner, commit to his judgment what *is* a lawful promise, what *is* a man's property; nor, however particular our directions become, can we possibly convey a direction at all otherwise than as he understands it.

The necessity of specifying moral rules in such a manner as to preclude, in the utmost possible degree, the abuses to which they would be liable from individual explanation, and also in such a manner as to insure that *concert* among numbers which is so often essential to the success of human undertakings, is the cause why we must make the specification of duty to be, in a great many cases, that of *simple submission* to the judgment of another party, who may have, if not more information, at least less bias.* However precise may be the rules we furnish beforehand to A. and B. for their conduct towards each other, and for the mode of their co-operation, where co-operation is necessary, they will never, even though conscientious, agree in the application of these rules. Their duty must be specified as *obedience* to C. ; —the duty of C. that of directing their actions in the cases submitted to him. This is the theory of the duty of *subordination;* and in this way it is, as we shall afterwards see, that the rights and obligations of *civil government* are deduced from the general principles of morals.

So much in regard to the effects of actions considered as forming species and classes.

* Still the *application* even of the rule of *submission,* must rest with him to whom the rule is given; and the *discretion* inevitably to be assumed by individuals in settling the question " to *whom* is submission to be given," in the cases of instituting or altering a mode of government, is the cause of the disorders that take place on such occasions.

Every action, however, whatever may be the species to which it belongs, may have some individual quality which distinguishes it from all others of that species. One lie, one theft may, of course, be less criminal than another lie, another theft—so of species in one class.

But it is to be carefully attended to, that the *individual* character belonging to any action of a species affects the obligation to avoid or perform such action only *as relative to other actions of that species;* that the *absolute* obligation, must, in every case, be according to that of the species; of the species, according to that of the genus; and so on. For it would be a contradiction in terms to say that an action could belong to a species which it was obligatory to perform, and yet that that action itself was not one which was thus obligatory. If "to tell a lie" is a *genus* of action which it is obligatory to avoid, then no good that a lie can ever effect, can make it allowable: though one that did produce a good effect, would certainly be *so far* more allowable than one that did not so: for, if a lie be, in any case, allowable, then the whole genus of the action, "to tell a lie," is not of obligation to be avoided, but only certain species of it, not comprehending such cases as supposed in the present instance. — In short, the obligation to perform, or avoid the performance of any action, as derived from the nature of its effects, is in the compound ratio of the effects of the individual action, and of the species, class, &c. to which it may belong.*

The reference to the *species* and *genus* of a moral action, which has now been described as necessary to be made, in order to estimate its moral character, is explained, by Dr. Thomas Brown, solely upon the principle of association. But really to say, as Dr. B. seems to have meant, that, in estimating the morality of a particular action—a petty theft for instance, — a consideration of the class to which it belongs only affects our judgment by our associating with the present feeling, the feeling which may have been derived from the view of other actions of the same class, seems to me much the same as to say that, in the value we put on a shilling, we do not make any reference to the value of silver as the *species* of substance of which it is made, but merely have that idea of its value which would arise from the consideration of any purpose of use or ornament it might serve, as an individual object, increased by association with the idea we may, on another occasion, have formed of the value of a splendid service of plate ; and increased, too, to the effect

* The objection started (and not, as I think, distinctly answered) by Paley, that it is unfair to throw upon one action the criminality of all others similar, is entirely removed by reflecting, that *degrees* of obligation are entirely relative; and that, if we multiply (so to speak) the obligation of any one action by the number of its species, we do the same in regard to all other actions with which that one is compared.

of unduly exaggerating, in our estimation, the value of the shilling. Surely when we say, generally, the shilling is an object of value, — besides meaning that it possesses an absolute value as opposed to the want of any value, - we may have a reference either to the value of this piece of silver, as compared with other pieces, or to that of the substance of which it is formed, as compared with other substances, or to both of these circumstances together. It is the same in estimating the moral character of an action, as, for instance, of an act of theft. If we say, — this theft is a bad one, — we mean it is bad as compared with other thefts ; if theft is a bad action — we speak of theft as of a class of actions. If we say generally — this action is a bad action — we may speak in reference either to the individual or to the class. But as no proposition regarding the morality of an action is *true at all* otherwise than *relatively* (that is, as between one individual and another of the same species — between one species and another of the same class) *unless it is true as a general proposition,* — whenever we pronounce absolutely of the moral character of an action, it is really not of an individual action that we speak, but of a species, genus, or class.

We may now shortly exemplify the manner in which, on the principles that have been exhibited, the morality of actions is computed.

An action being *specified*, the question is,—would this action, as *specified*, produce fit, or unfit effects, or neither? According to the answer, the action will be obligatory, or the contrary, or indifferent. The next step is to abstract the circumstance or circumstances which distinguish this individual action from others similar to it, and with which it formed a species; and then to try whether or not, as *the representative of this species*, its effects retain the same character.

Supposing that they do, we proceed to abstract the specific and generic character; till what may be predicated of the action, may be done in the most general form of it to which the predicate will apply.

It may be, however, that the individual produces fit effects, the species produces fit effects, but the genus, i. e. the whole genus, does not : certain species producing bad effects. The result in this case would be, that certain species of the action would be pronounced obligatory or allowable, others not so. But, from the causes adverted to in the former part of this chapter, a question may arise whether or not the species that we should pronounce obligatory or allowable, are so clearly distinguished from those which are pronounced not so, as to afford a chance of their not being confounded by the ignorance or self-deceit of those on whom the obligation is laid, and who have to determine its import. In other words, to permit certain species may be equivalent to the permission of the genus; making the only other alternative, to forbid the whole genus: and the determination of this point will depend on the circumstance, which of these alternatives, if adopted, would be attended with most fit or fewest unfit effects: and it is to be held in view, that every moral injunction must, in its nature, have unfit effects thus far, that it obliges men to act otherwise than they would spontaneously do: thus imposing some trouble or difficulty, or the denying of some gratification.*

* In judging of the correctness of the system of moral obligation which I am exhibiting, I am anxious that regard should be had to the difference between *forming* rules, and *applying* them. It is only the former I am concerned with. As an instance of this difference, I have here occasion to observe, that a *maxim* which, used in explaining and applying the rules of morality, is most valuable and important, is by no means an unexceptionable principle in the formation of such rules : I mean the maxim — " where there is *doubt* if an action be lawful, abstain from it:"—An admirable maxim for the man, for the agent; not so much so for the moralist, for the lawgiver : if we mean that where the one is to abstain, the other is to prohibit. In laying down moral rules, there is sometimes as great a danger in too much straitening, as in too much relaxing the bonds. If, in the latter case, they may give too much room, in the former they may burst, and be ineffectual altogether. A man who doubts whether or not he may with propriety go to the theatre, should *not* go. A moralist who doubts whether he would *allow* going to the theatre — should *consider* his judgment.

As an example, let the action specified be, "playing a game at chess, as an occasional recreation, and without a stake." No one would probably say that this could have bad effects. Abstract the *individual* character of the game, and leave as its *species*, "any game of skill" — still there will appear no bad effects. Take away successively the circumstances,—" occasionally,"—" of skill" — " for no stake :" — each successive abstraction will make the truth of the remaining position more questionable : and the general term " playing a game," or "*gaming*," standing for a *class*, without restriction of frequency, sort, or stake, — will express an action which no one would allow to be of harmless effects. " Playing a game," then, is a *genus* of action, of which certain *species* would produce fit, or no unfit effects, other species unfit. Two different views will now be taken of the case, by different moralists. One may say, many games afford an innocent recreation, and refresh the mind for more laborious exertions ; some sharpen the intellect; all maintain an agreeable excitation of the spirits, and give variety to social intercourse ; more unfit effects, then, would result from the entire prohibition, than could be produced by any extension of a precept allowing certain *species* of gaming. Another would argue thus : let a man play at chess, and there is no reason why he may not play at backgammon, quadrille, whist, any game. Let him play for a shilling, and you cannot prevent a guinea being staked. Let him play once a month, and he will come to play every night; and at last may bring upon himself all the misery that generally befals the professed gambler. Gaming is, farther, but as one species of dissolute conduct, and will carry all the rest along with it.—This argument is obviously founded on the difficulty or impossibility of *defining* the allowable, so as to separate them from the unallowable *species*.

The difficulty which is felt in determining many questions of practical right or duty, exists, for the most part, not in regard to the particular proposition that may chance to be under discussion, but in regard to that proposition, taken as a general truth, the representative only of a great many others; in other words, we are not so much at a loss to decide whether this right, that obligation exists, in the individual case before us; as whether or not it exists only under certain specialities belonging to that case, or may exist without them. Each of the parties carrying on the dispute generalizes the proposition, in his own mind, to a different extent from what the other does; and thus they may both be right in expressing contrary views. As predicating of a genus, the proposition may be false; as of a species, true.

Even if the parties were at one, as to the true extent of meaning in which the proposition might actually hold good, they might still contest its suitableness as a *practical rule* of morality, upon the point of how far it would be, in practice, *understood* and *applied* in its true extent.

There always exists a reason why every disputed or new case should be brought within any received and acknowledged rule of morality to which it may most easily be referred, rather than that it should be made an exception from that rule, and a special rule formed for that occasion, or for similar occasions ; because the very liberty of admitting exceptions, in any case, to the ordinary rules of morality, must be liable to dangerous abuse.

A few circumstances are now to be pointed out which affect the obligatoriness of actions, *individually* considered.

I. To say that any effect, fit in itself, is well or ill produced, is just to say that such effect is so much the more or less fit, and consequently that it is more or less obligatory on any agent to act so as it may be produced. To cure a broken leg is fit ; especially to do it well, so that no trace of the accident may remain : to do it ill, that is, merely to remove the pain, or to prevent its causing death, yet so as that the patient remains lame, is also fit, but less so. If one man can produce the first effect, another only the second, it is more obligatory on the first to perform the cure, than on the second.

II. In estimating the effect of an action, we must include every thing of a fit or unfit nature that takes place in consequence of that action, or which, but for it, would not have taken place.

Thus the pleasure or pain arising to the *agent* from the performance of the action, is as much a part of the whole effect, as what merely affects the subject of an action.· If the same effect, as regards the subject of the action, can be produced by one agent only with a great deal of pain, uneasiness, or inconvenience to himself, and by another without any pain or inconvenience at all, but perhaps with actual gratification, the whole effect of the action, performed by the first, must be less fit than in the other case ; and consequently the latter must be under the greater obligation to perform the action.

A surgeon who lives next door to a patient may, without the least trouble, relieve an uneasiness he may be suffering ; which is so much positive good produced : another who should come a dozen miles for the purpose, may suffer more from fatigue, than the patient would suffer for want of him.

The two remarks just stated are in general to this effect, that when a fit action can be performed by different persons, it is most obligatory on him who can perform it best and most easily.

The peculiar obligation that relationship creates, receives an increase from both the sources now enumerated. We perform a duty best to those whom

we love; we do it with less irksomeness to ourselves : because so far from its being painful to
perform it, it would be painful to be restrained
from the performance.

But independently of these circumstances, if some
individuals were marked out, even by an arbitrary
sign or mark, as the peculiar care of certain other
individuals, it is evident that more beneficial effects
would be produced in this way, than if the good
offices of each particular agent were to be dissi-
pated over the general mass of his fellow creatures.*

To the two observations now illustrated may be
added this, that an effect, along with any peculiar
fitness belonging to itself, may be the cause of
another effect that is fit; and will in consequence
become so far more obligatory. Thus even if it
were not intrinsically fit that merit should be rewarded, or that guilt should be punished, that a
promise should be fulfilled to the person to whom it
has been made, or that a favour should be requited to the one who has conferred it; yet these effects, being made part of an established order of
things, and in such a manner as to be calculated
upon as what would constantly and invariably take
place, would obviously become the causes of other
fit effects; by repressing wickedness, promoting
virtue and benevolence, and increasing mutual

* Hence the doctrines of Godwin are not to be viewed as
furnishing objections to the principle of general utility : being
merely erroneous deductions from that principle.

confidence. — It is necessary for me, however, to protest against the supposition that this consideration is to be taken as either the sole, or primary ground of the obligations now enumerated.

Lastly — When the effect of an action is uncertain, it must of course be estimated according to the chances. Thus if there are two chances to one that an action will not produce a given effect, or that such effect will be produced without it, the effect of the action is only as half the given effect, and the obligation to perform such action in proportion. If two men fall into a situation of danger, one of whom has some chance, the other none to save himself, there is a greater obligation to assist the latter than the former; or if, instead of their chance of escape being unequal, the chance of saving them be so—if one can certainly be saved, the other not certainly—the former ought to be assisted in preference.*

Enough has now been offered to illustrate and confirm the general principle, that, in proportion as the effects of any action, (the effects produced by that action, and which would not be produced without it,) whether taken as an individual, or as representing a species, or a class, are fit, or unfit, there exists obligation to perform or avoid that action; nor would it seem that any thing more could possibly be necessary to make it right or wrong to perform an action. It appears to me

* Many of the truths relating to *duty*, stated in this section,

accordingly, that all the rules of morality may be
deduced from this principle, and that this principle is of itself sufficient, without any other, to
explain these rules. Of that however which I
comprehend under the description of the fit, and
unfit effects of an action, an important part has
yet to be exhibited; the consideration of which
will, I trust, be found to fill up any deficiency,
with which the foregoing statement may appear
to be chargeable.

SECT. II.

Of SPECIAL *Obligations, as arising from the* circumstantial *and* derived *Effects of Actions.*

THAT description of *effects* from which the obligation of actions has been derived, in the preceding
Section, is what I call the *proper* effects of an
action; and includes, first, the sort or amount of
pleasure or happiness which it is the nature of any
action to create, either absolutely, or in relation to
something in the situation of the *subject* of the
action, that makes an effect of this nature more
valuable to him; next, the *perfection in degree,*
with which the effect is accomplished; and lastly,

are, in themselves, too trite to be offered either as morally in-
structive or philosophically interesting. Their only purpose is
to exemplify the universality of application that belongs to the
principle, as explaining every possible rise or fall, increase or
diminution of moral obligation.

the pleasure or ease with which the *agent* performs the action.

It must be exceedingly clear, that, in whatever degree an action is attended with fit consequences or effects in any or in all of these ways, it must be so far obligatory, right, or proper, to perform such an action ; or that there exists, so far, in the nature of things, a reason for the performance of it.   Nor is it possible, under any circumstances,—whether the action may in other ways have unfit effects, or other fit effects of a different kind, — but that the fitness of its *proper* effects must always affect, in some degree, the obligation which may on the whole exist, either as to the performance or omission of it ; and can never be entirely negatived by any other kind of fitness.

But the obligation under which an agent is placed to perform a particular action, depends only in part upon the fitness of the *proper* effect of that action. — Why my father, child, brother, benefactor, acquaintance, neighbour, or why any one to whom I have made a promise, should enjoy any particular benefit more than any other person, there exists, as regards the positive degree of benefit rendered, no reason whatever : but why *I*, rather than any other person, should do good to those who may stand in any of these relations towards me, rather than that I should do so to others, there does exist reason.   In other words, an action productive of good, may be equally *fit* to be done, as regards its proper effect, whether to my benefactor, or to any other man ; but it is not equally *obligatory* on me to do it.

Another distinct source of obligation then, yet to be pointed out, is that which is drawn from what I shall call the *circumstantial* effects of an action. In the first place, certain effects, positively *unfit*, sometimes arise from the mere non-performance of actions that would, if performed, produce positively fit effects ; and secondly, additional unfit effects, of a different kind from those which properly belong to an action, are sometimes the consequence of such action ; and this, in both cases, from certain circumstances of *relation* between the agent and the subject of the action, by which the latter must nourish a dependence upon the agent's performing the action, in the one case, and avoiding it, in the other.

The circumstances out of which this dependence originates are only, I believe, the three following : Where the agent is bound by natural affection ; by a promise ; or by the receipt of a favour.

First. Whenever an agent must be believed, from the constitution of our nature, to bear a particular affection towards another being, that being must form some sort of *dependence* on the kindness and favour of such agent. The mere omission, then, of acts producing positive good towards near relations, neighbours, countrymen, benefactors, produces positive pain and uneasiness ;

because it disappoints an expectation founded on a knowledge of the human constitution. To which it is to be added, that, as the affection in such cases is always reciprocal, that is, as the agent is not only presumed and expected to bear good will to the subjects of the action, but is himself viewed with more or less affection by them, they must, as bearing him affection, be more wounded by his indifference, than by the same indifference displayed on the part of others. Not to receive a return of affection from those to whom we bear affection, is itself a positive pain.

Secondly. An agent who makes a *promise* to another, necessarily excites in him an expectation of receiving some good or desirable thing that is promised; for without this, it would not be a promise. By non-fulfilment of the promise, he deprives the person of the thing expected; thereby producing an effect positively unfit.*

If one man destroys another's crop of grain or fruit, or if he intercepts a present destined for him, the immorality of such an act appears to us to stand on clear grounds — as clear as that of robbing or maiming the person: yet there is no more difficulty in explaining the obligation of a promise, than the obligation of not injuring our neighbour's crop. In both cases, we deprive him of only an *expected* good. All the difference is, that the act

* Ax. XXIII.

by which this unfit effect is produced, is, as regards the agent, *negative* in the one case, where it is *positive* in the other, and *vice versa*. In the case of destroying a neighbour's crop, the expectation has been *produced without* the act of the agent, the expectation is disappointed *by his act*. In the case of a promise, the expectation is produced *by the act;* the disappointment, *without* an act. In neither case would the unfit effect take place, but by an *act* of the agent. It is therefore as obligatory to avoid the *omission* by which the *effect* is produced, in the one case, as the *commission* by which it is produced, in the other.

To some people this explication may appear to leave the main difficulty untouched; and they will ask why does the *promisee* expect the performance of the promise? Now this appears to me just the same sort of question as it would be to ask a mathematician, who had demonstrated that the angles contained in a three-sided figure were equal to two right angles, — why the figure should have three sides? He would answer,—this is my hypothesis : — so answers the moral theorist. A promise is, in its very nature and essence, a certain act by which one person conveys to another an expectation and belief that he will do him some good. This I take to be not a proposition regarding a promise, but the very definition of a promise. The expectation of the promisee, in short, does not presuppose the obligation of the promise; but the obligation of the promise presupposes the expectation of the promisee.

The account now given of the obligation of a promise, is entirely different from that given by Price and some others, — who resolve a breach of promise into a *violation of truth*, in so far as the promiser makes the affirmation contained in the promise to turn out *false*. But that breach of promise is different from breach of truth, and that even were it otherwise, it is the disappointment of an expectation, not the deceit, that is the specific moral wrong, may be shewn by a very simple illustration. If I say, I shall wear a white hat next week, and wear a black one, nobody would accuse me either of breach of promise, or of falsehood, (though certainly I make my affirmation untrue:) because neither, on the one hand, is any body disappointed in the expectation of any good; nor, on the other, was the signification of my intention to wear a white hat necessarily an untruth, in so far as it may have expressed a sincere intention. But if I promise to make any man a present of a hat, and fail in doing so; or say I wore a white hat last Sunday, when in fact I wore a black one, I break a promise, because I disappoint an expectation, in the one case; and utter what I know to be untrue, or tell a falsehood, in the other.

The obligation to speak truth presupposes a man's belief in what he is told, in the same way as the obligation to keep a promise made to him, presupposes his belief in the promise. In neither case, of course, is the belief to be explained from the obligation, but the former must be assumed in explaining the latter. Why a man believes either a simple affirmation, or a promise, is a question that bears no more relation to the present inquiry, than why a man believes that his son or his brother bears an affection towards him, or that his fields or his orchard will bear a crop. We believe both the affirmations and promises of others long before we have any idea of moral obligation at all, and this tendency to believe others, seems, like that to speak truth ourselves, an ultimate fact in our constitution: though no doubt the principle is afterwards strengthened by a perception of moral obligation, and the confidence we may have in its influence over others.

Thirdly. The obligation of *gratitude* differs from the obligation of a promise, less in kind, than in degree. There is no reason why the mere acceptance of a favour should not, as an *act*, be just as significant of an engagement, on the part of the person benefited, to make some sort of return, as, in other cases, a nod, or a few detached and unconnected words may be.

A promise does not require an explicit verbal statement of the intentions of the promiser. The essence of a promise, and that which makes it morally binding, is simply this, that the promiser knowingly conveys an expectation to the promisee, that he will render him something good or desirable; or rather that he performs some act, which by common usage and consent, is so far understood. * The question is, then, is the acceptance of a favour so understood?

Now nothing can be more clear than that there is no case in which a man would accept a favour, reckoned by himself as such, that he would not, rather than lose it, engage *generally* to requite it, or do some good in return for it. But what it is certain, judging from the ordinary principles of human conduct, that a man would always do, if required, on receiving a favour, it may be presumed that he actually does, by accepting the favour. Just in the same way a man who accepts any office is held, by *that act*, to *promise* the performance of the duties of it; and why? Because no man would accept an office without being ready to make such a promise, if required. And, in general, when an agent performs any act that is favourable to us, or evinces his confidence or favourable opinion, — but the doing of which he might have

---

* I am doubtful of the correctness of Paley's rule about the interpretation of promises — namely, that they are to be interpreted in that sense in which the promiser understood the promisee to receive them. Is the promisee liable to suffer disappointment, because the promiser may not have attached that meaning to the promise which common usage would assign to it?

avoided until he had exacted a promise, binding us to some condition in return,— the performance of such act on his part is taken as imposing the force of a promise on us, unless we *forbid* or *resist* the performance of the act, or *explicitly* protest against the implied engagement. Thus, in all those cases where a man is said to put himself in another's power, by leaving to him the terms of a bargain, by entrusting him with a secret which he might turn to his disadvantage, and the like, we reckon the person thus trusted in, under a peculiar obligation not to misuse the confidence. When a criminal offers to plead guilty, the judge thinks it necessary to warn him that it will not save him from punishment: thus evincing his feeling that the acceptance of the prisoner's voluntary confession is itself an act inferring some obligation not to turn it to his disadvantage, unless such obligation be *expressly disclaimed :* and it is quite clear that the acceptance of a favour always conveys, in the same way as in these instances, a *general promise* to make a return.

The representation now given is entirely confirmed by the forms of expression in which favours are either asked or acknowledged, which are, to all intents and purposes, promises. " If you will do this, I shall be *obliged* to you "—" under an *obligation* to you"—" I shall take it as a favour"—" you have laid me under an obligation"—" I am bound to you for ever " — and so forth. Does any one

doubt that these are *promises?* and that they may
be conveyed by a look or a gesture, or by the mere
receipt of the favour, as much as by words?

But, even without supposing the act of accepting a favour to be the conveyance of a promise to
make requital, we may, to a certain extent, deduce the duty of requiting a favour from a principle of simple distributive justice. For the most
part, he who confers a favour incurs some trouble
or sacrifice, more or less, in doing so. He who
receives the favour then, receives some good, at
some degree of cost to another. That he should,
in his turn, and he rather than any other person,
submit to some sacrifice for the sake of recom-
pensing that by which he and not any other was
formerly benefited, is nothing more than what is
fit as a just equalization of good and evil among
different beings.

It often happens, too, that there is moral *desert*
in the act by which a benefit is conferred. The
obligation to reward desert (which however is
general on every moral agent) forms an addition
to that which would otherwise have lain on the
person benefited, to recompense the benefactor.

The obligation of gratitude depends in part
also upon a similar principle to that of natural affection, — since gratitude is itself a natural affection. To do good to one who has done good to
us, is obligatory, because natural; and being natural, must be expected; and being expected, the

failure of it is not merely the omitting to do a good, but must occasion positive pain and disappointment. Add to which, that, as a benefactor must possess more or less affection towards the person benefited, the failure of a duty on the part of the latter must naturally be more keenly felt.

When one being, then, has benefited another, he cannot but expect a return of the benefit, just as he cannot but expect the fulfilment of a promise. The obligation is, in each case, an obligation *not to disappoint the expectation.* The great difference is, that, in the one case, the expectation is *specific ;* in the other, it is only *general.*

It now becomes necessary to explain how the morality of actions is to be calculated where different obligations contend ; that is, for the most part, general with special, public with private obligations.

To cases of this description some of the first principles of morals have direct application, particularly the Axioms No. 5, 6, 8, 11 : — instances may sometimes occur, however, in which none of those principles may be altogether sufficient to solve the difficulty.

Generally speaking, obligations are found to contend in every case where the observance of a moral rule is attended with the permission or production of any evil, of any pain or uneasiness, any unfit effect ;—for undoubtedly there is always an obligation to avoid the permission or production of evil. In this general mode of speaking, there are opposing duties in those cases where we may prevent any evil by falsehood or fraud — as when we may save an innocent man by giving false evidence, or relieve the distress of a poor man by cheating a rich man. But whenever a general rule of conduct comes to be established, and when we are once satisfied that such rule must be strictly observed without regard to consequences, such cases cease to be considered as cases of opposing duty; for the balance being once struck *for* the rule, *against* the exception, all the obligation thenceforth lies with the former, none with the latter; so that there ceases to be any opposition. The fact is, then, that what is called a case of opposing obligations just means a doubtful, undetermined case ;—there cannot otherwise, properly speaking, exist a case of opposing obligations. The stronger obligation extinguishes the weaker.*

The general rules then that have already been given for computing the morality of actions, are all that can be given in regard to cases of opposing duties ; — or rather it might be said that all

* Extinguishes it *absolutely* — it can never, in theory, do so *relatively*. — Absolutely, I am under an obligation to avoid giving false evidence in a court of justice, in every case. If false evidence would prevent injustice, I am nevertheless bound to avoid giving false evidence ; if false evidence would produce injustice, I can be no more than bound to avoid it. But, relatively speaking, I am surely under a *greater* obligation to avoid falsehood in the one case than in the other.

rules for computing the morality of actions are, in their very nature, rules for cases of opposing duties. For whenever we ask, — is such an action lawful or not? — it must be an action which will answer some beneficial purpose to ourselves or others, otherwise we should not ask such a question regarding it ; and so far as it is beneficial, it is, in relative degree, obligatory ; while, on the other hand, our asking such a question shews that we at least suspect it is not entirely harmless in all other respects. The mode then, as we have seen, in which we ascertain its lawfulness, is by considering the nature of its effects as an individual, or as representing a species, a genus, or a class. If the whole species, genus, and class of the action produces no unfit effects, of course our inquiry is at an end. If the genus is mischievous, the species beneficial, the question comes to be,— does this species possess grounds of exception from the general rule, not belonging to other species? — If these grounds exist, and can be *sufficiently defined*, the species of action is lawful, though not the genus. — Now every case of opposing duties is just one involving a question whether the circumstances composing the obligation to perform the one action, form a *special* ground of exception from the general rule applicable to the other. Thus if a public and private duty are opposed, either the reasons for performing the private duty form a species of cases excepted from

s 2

the general rule applicable to the public duty; or, *vice versa,* the reasons for performing the public duty form a species of cases to be excepted from the rule applicable to the private duty. If I am under an obligation to deliver up my benefactor to public justice, this is a special exception from the general duty of gratitude, or, which is the same thing, the duty of gratitude is not a special exception from the rule of public duty; or, on the other hand, if I am under an obligation to preserve my benefactor, the duty of gratitude is here a special exception from the rule of public duty; or, which is the same thing, the public duty is not an exception from the rule of gratitude. Now the determination of this question resolves entirely into a calculation of the beneficial or hurtful effects which result from preserving the rule, or sustaining the exception, in the one case or in the other.

As already observed, what are called cases of opposing duties are all cases which do not admit of being clearly resolved; — for when they do admit of being clearly resolved, they cease to be cases of opposing duties.

Some writers have expressed themselves to the effect that such cases as now spoken of can only be determined by *immediate feeling.* If this expression only means that, whereas it is impossible to form a general rule applicable to such cases, the agent must be determined by what at the moment he feels to be right (using the word *feels* as a general expression for thinks, reckons, judges should be done, — chooses or inclines to do) the assertion is little more than a truism, namely — that a man must determine as he sees fit to determine. If it means that we have some instinctive feeling to guide us correctly in such cases, — I must deny, or at least not admit the fact. Whatever the expression means, however, I have found it used, if I mistake not, sometimes to justify the inference that *reason* cannot determine between right and wrong, — sometimes the inference that the beneficial or hurtful *effects* of actions are not that from which their morality is computed. Now in this way it might just as well be said that to guess the result of a particular throw of the dice is a matter of immediate feeling, a matter not coming within the province of reason, a matter not to be determined by the laws of motion and forces. It is undoubtedly true that reason cannot, by an application of the laws of motion and forces, tell us how the dice will turn up; but this happens, not because all the turns of the dice and their final position of rest are not determined by the laws of motion and forces—not because reason is incapable of discovering and applying those laws, but because there are not data, in the particular case, on which to found the application. So, in cases of doubtful morality, it is not because the beneficial or hurtful consequences of an action are not the grounds of its being morally right or wrong — not because reason cannot discern that it is right or wrong on account of its having such consequences — that we cannot form a precise determination; but because the consequences of each of the two actions respectively, standing for species and classes, do not admit of being measured or compared. Here, as in the other case, we are assured of the truth of the rule, we are assured of the ability of reason to discover and apply the rule, but we want the data.*

It is not often, in theory at least, that any species or genus of action can be pronounced of absolute and universal obligation; since we can almost always suppose an opposing duty to occur that may form a case of exception. In practice, however, there are some rules justly held of para-

---

* A condemnation that has been passed by many of the most judicious authors upon *casuistry*, or the study of what is called cases of conscience, is most fully warranted, if casuistry is considered as a *practical talent or habit*. It is a happy and just remark, — I think, of Mr Dugald Stewart's, — that there are some people whom no consideration whatever would induce to do wrong, who will yet never discover any thing to be wrong, or be at a loss to justify it as right, which they are inclined to do. But however much and justly the employment of casuistry in the regulation of conduct is to be discouraged, the consideration of extreme hypothetical cases is often necessary for theoretical purposes, and for discovering and establishing the general principles on which the rules of morality are founded.

mount obligation; that is, which do not admit of being opposed by a stronger : such as not to murder, to steal, to lie. These are whole genera which are of obligation to avoid — having no specific exceptions; and here we are to say, — this it is our duty to avoid, be the consequence what it will.

Wherever, in regard to cases of opposing duties, special moral rules have been established, they have been established either upon an experimental or a prospective application of the principles described. So far as, in any case, it is impossible, either from experience or general reasoning, to apply these principles, so far the moral rule in regard to such case must be disputable and uncertain : but the arguments on either side will always be found to proceed on these principles.

After the obligation of any action (meaning the obligation either to perform or avoid such action) has been estimated by the rules above delivered, from a view of both the proper and circumstantial effects of such action; and after this obligation has been compared with other contending obligations, and the resulting one, or the obligation on the whole, established, there yet remains a secondary species of obligation to be considered : secondary as regards the mode of its derivation, but far from unimportant as regards its nature. — Whenever it is obligatory on an agent to do any thing to another agent, the latter has a *right* that it should be done; or when it is obligatory on one agent to avoid doing something to another, the former has no *right* to do it, and the latter has a *right* that it should not be done. If an agent does to another what he has no right to do, or does not do what the other has a right to have done, the latter suffers an *injury*.

The reception of an *injury* creates a species of pain entirely distinct from that of either the proper or circumstantial effects of the action which occasions it.

If I wilfully throw a stone upon, and break, a man's leg, the pain, and loss of the limb, is the *evil:* which would be the same if the stone had fallen on it by accident. But how different is the amount of suffering in this last case, from what it would be where there is a consciousness that such suffering has been produced by the wanton unnecessary cruelty of a moral intelligent agent? The sense of *injury* is yet more insupportable than the physical evil.

If I break a promise, the *evil* consists in the disappointment of expectation: which evil is alike experienced, where the disappointment has been the effect of undesigning physical agency — as when the weather destroys a crop, on the value of which the farmer had calculated. The consciousness of the disappointment's being caused by wilful breach of obligation, on the part of another, is a cause of distress essentially distinct from the disappointment itself.

The obligation not to break a man's leg, arises from the unfitness of the *proper* effect of an action : the obligation to keep a promise, from the unfitness of the *circumstantial* effect of an action, i. e. of breaking the promise. The pain created by the *sense of injury*, is as real a pain as that of the physical hurt, in the one case, or the disappointed hope, in the other ; but perfectly distinct from both of these, and the source of a new and real obligation ; which, however it may combine and coalesce with the original one, cannot exist originally of itself ; but presupposes another obligation, having an independent existence and source of its own. It is obligatory not to commit an injury : but the very notion of *injury* implies a *previous* obligation, of which it is the violation.

There must be certain original sources of pleasure or pain, before any emotions or feelings can exist at all. To these emotions or feelings, however, as being themselves pleasures or pains, the same predicates apply, (namely, that they are *fit*— the production of them *obligatory*,—or vice versa,) as to the original pleasures or pains, without the previous existence of which these feelings could never have arisen ; and thus the pain of injury, arising from the *wrong* infliction of another original and primary sort of pain, is unfit, and the causing of it injurious, in addition to the original injury: and so on, *ad infinitum.* This is another case, along with others occurring through this work, falling under the *second* remark subjoined to the axioms in p. 203. It is almost needless to observe that the specific pain which arises from the sense of *injury,* can only be felt by a *moral* being.

The distinction between the pain of *injury,* and the pain in the infliction of which the injury itself consists, has by no means been sufficiently observed; and, in consequence, some inquirers, fixing their view on the former, to the exclusion of the latter, (in the same way as they have looked at the excellence and desirableness of virtue, without perceiving the mode in which virtue comes, in any case, to exist,) have been led to object to the justest accounts of the ultimate sources of our moral notions.

It is to be observed that the consideration of the pain of *injury* has no place, where obligations *contend,* till after the comparative weight of the contending obligations has been fixed. If I have made an unlawful promise, and then refuse to keep it, the party affected cannot properly be said to be *injured,* though he suffers the pain of disappointment by my refusal to fulfil the promise; because the refusal being, on the whole, obligatory on me, he has not, on the whole, the right to have the promise kept, and cannot suffer the peculiar pain of *injury,* which arises from the sense of a right's being violated.

Strictly analogous to the pain of injury, is what may be called the pain of *injustice:* by which I mean the painful feeling with which we are affected in regard to one who obtains an advantage or enjoyment at the expense of suffering or deprivation to ourselves : and this even when the act which causes the injustice, may be that of a third party.

It has already appeared, that our ideas of *moral fitness* require, not merely that we should be happy rather than miserable, but that we should not be less happy, or more miserable, than are others of equal desert. It seems to us in an especial degree unfit that we should be positively miserable, while others, of less, or not of greater desert, are positively happy. But the painful sense of unfitness is exasperated to the highest possible degree, when the inequality is produced by actual transference—when the enjoyment of another is caused by our suffering, or, (which are but cases of this,) when we suffer a punishment due to another, or another obtains a reward due to us. In cases like these last, we cannot but look upon the one who profits at our expense, as being, in effect, even though not in act, the *cause* or *occasion* of our suffering. And though the painful sentiment we experience in regard to the person who thus obtains an unjust advantage over us, differs entirely from resentment, (indeed it is not properly a feeling *towards* him, but a feeling in

regard to the relative situation of him and ourselves, considered as an *effect*) it is one of exquisite pain. Resentment, as arising from the
sense of injury, can exist only towards the *agency*
by which the injustice is effected.

It is evident that, in regard to the circumstantial
and derived effects of actions, the same truth
applies that was formerly stated in regard to
the proper effects : namely, that in whatever
degree unfit effects of any or all the kinds called circumstantial or derived, (which from their
nature must usually be unfit,) attend the omission
or commission of an action, it is obligatory so far
not to omit or commit that action.

And in general, and under all possible circumstances, the rule must hold good, that in proportion as any effect is, in its own nature, fit to be
produced, there exists a reason for the performance
of the action by which it may be produced ; and
vice versa with regard to unfit effects. Even if
we should suppose other grounds of obligation,
they could never negative this one, or exclude it
from having its proper influence.

We may now remark the precise point at which,
in the formation of a specific moral proposition,
necessary truth, as visible *a priori*, ends ; and
opinion, as derived from observation and experience, begins.

Such proposition is the conclusion of a syllogism; of which the major is a necessary truth, the minor *generally* an opinion.*

That an action which produces fit effects is so far obligatory, is a truth that rests on the same foundation as any of Euclid's axioms. That this or that sort of action will actually produce fit effects, may be either certainly true, or certainly false, but not *necessarily* either.

We may observe that practical moralists generally adopt a different mode of classification, when enumerating what it is our duty to do, and what it is our duty to avoid. When enumerating duties, they specify duties to parents, to children, to neighbours, &c. When enumerating crimes, they do not specify them thus, crimes against parents, against children, &c., but crimes against the person, against the property, against the mind. The reason of this is because positive duties are, comparatively speaking, obligatory only in regard to particular persons; the obligation not to commit crimes is general: consequently, in the one case, we look to the object of the action; in the other, to the nature of it.

* When I speak of an *opinion*, it is not as of what must be less *certainly* true; but as, in logical classification, a truth of a different species.

CHAPTER IV.

THEORY OF CIVIL GOVERNMENT.

THE question to be investigated regarding *civil government* is, — how any individual or number of individuals in a community have a right forcibly to control the actions of each of the remaining members of that community : the persons controlled not being inferior, it may be superior, to those who exercise the control, in wisdom and virtue, and even, (setting aside the interference of third parties,) in physical strength:—or how there exists, on any member of a community, a *moral* obligation, (independently of compulsion,) to submit to such control; often against his own judgment and inclination, and where, in denying such submission, he might yet be violating no positive right otherwise existing ?

That certain members of a community *ought*, or *have a right*, to control the remaining members, — that the latter *ought* to submit to the control of the former, —are, in form and matter, moral rules or precepts, propositions expressive of duty.   To deduce these rules then, in the ordinary manner, from the general principles of morals, is to explain, in the way required, the *theory of government.*

It will be at once acknowledged that most beneficial effects arise from the use of this control,—that most pernicious effects are prevented by it. It will be acknowledged as what is clearly expedient or desirable, in the same way as it might be expedient and desirable to deprive a spendthrift of the fortune he is wasting in vice and folly, and to divide it among the poor. But the *beneficial* results of forcible control, though admitted, are still supposed insufficient to account for the *right* of control, any more than the beneficial results that might sometimes arise from one man's violent interference in the domestic concerns of another, could justify the use of such interference, — more especially if provoked by no positive wrong committed on the other part. In short, this appears to come under that description of cases in which a clear right is sacrificed to a point of expediency.

Such is the difficulty. With a view to its solution, let it be observed,—

I. That, setting aside the right of compulsion in governors, and supposing all the members of a community disposed to fulfil, without compulsion, every moral obligation that could be shewn to lie upon them, a moral obligation would exist upon a community to submit to the directions of some governing head. Even supposing every man willing, to the best of his means and judgment, to promote such objects as should be necessary for the safety or prosperity of the community, and to be perfectly just and innocuous (as he might consider just and innocuous) towards other individuals, it is obvious that without a system of subordination, i. e. without individuals', to a certain extent, giving up their private judgment, neither could public designs be accomplished, nor private injuries avoided. Public designs require *concert ;* private differences require *neutral adjudication —* let the mere intentions of individuals be ever so good. But both concert and neutral adjudication suppose submission to a guiding head — which is the essential notion of *government.**

It is indispensable to the right understanding of the theory of government, that we clearly apprehend, in the first instance, the existence of a moral rule of obligation (even setting compulsion aside) binding, or at least permitting, some men to direct, binding others to obey : and of this rule specifically taken, and considered not merely as distinct from, but as additional to, or rather as so far superseding, any more general obligation merely to

* It will of course be understood that the question is here treated entirely in the abstract, on the assumption that there ought to be a government of some kind or other, some degree of submission to it more or less; the particular kind of the one or degree of the other is here of no consequence.

practise justice, and assist in the furtherance of public designs. In other words, it requires to be distinctly seen that, in the present circumstances of mankind, it is not enough, it does not satisfy all the claims of moral *duty*, that a man merely, to the best of his own judgment, does no ill, or even, on the contrary, attempts to do good; unless, along with this, nay sometimes in contradiction to his own views of what is right to be done, he bears a part in a system of subordination to authority, in which different portions of the community respectively command and obey: there being certain indispensable ends that can be attained by this *specific* mode of conduct, and by no other modes whatsoever.

But, secondly—If we can once evince a man to be under a specific moral obligation, as a means of effecting good not otherwise attainable, to bear part in a system of subordination, i. e. not merely to avoid doing harm, or even to do good, according to his own views, but, if required, in the nature of his circumstances or situation in society, to render a simple obedience, — if we can evince this (whether it may be compelled or not) to be something, at least, *morally right*, proper, reasonable, what ought to be, — then to this case the moral axiom becomes applicable that " whatever a moral agent is under an obligation to do, it is, or may be, fit, or not unfit, that he should be *compelled* to do"*—whence it follows that others may have a *right* to use such compulsion, and that he has no (absolute) right why it should not be used. If this is the case, (which will soon be more fully illustrated,) the exercise of control will be fit, not only as regards the general effects of such exercise, but fit, or not unfit, as regards the immediate subject of it.

It cannot fail to be observed, however, that the establishment of the principle of subordination only removes one step farther off, the very difficulty which the principle is resorted to for overcoming. Subordination we found necessary for purposes of concert and adjudication of differences; but for the determination of such questions as — who are to be rulers, who subjects ?— how far are the powers of the former, the submission of the latter to extend? — there must appear to be, at least, as much need of concert and adjudication as there can possibly be in regard to the primary purposes for which a system of subordination is required : and it must be owned that the most specific answers which these questions can be made to receive, the most specific principles that can be laid down on this subject, will still be of such a kind, that their application, by individual judgment, (to which we must come at last,) will, at first sight, appear to carry no less mischief along with it, than that which the appointment of a

* Ax. IX.

governing authority at all is devised to prevent. Neither is there any rule which we can imagine men to agree upon, as to how such an appointment is to be made; nor, if such rule could be agreed on, can we suppose that men would ever agree in the application of it. The use of force by him who judges himself to be the ruler, and as such, to have the right of using force, will be met by the similar use of force on the part of those who judge that he is not the ruler; and the question still comes back upon us, whether greater danger will not arise from the use of individual judgment in these cases, than in those other cases which it is the object of a constituted authority to withdraw from its exercise.

Now fact and experience decide this question in the negative, to this effect, namely, that less evil is produced, on the whole, by all the ignorance, the selfishness, the injustice, and violence of mankind, in the application of this moral rule, — some are to command, others are to obey — than in the application of any system of rules of conduct that could possibly be devised, *not involving the principle of subordination.* — We are here placed under a necessity of adopting one or other of these three courses: first, specifying the various duties of men in general, (including that of civil obedience,) to leave every one to apply such specification, and act according to it or not, as he pleases; secondly, to specify, in addition, as a

duty on all, that of compelling others to do their
duty; or thirdly, to specify this additional duty
as only belonging to rulers. Whatever abuse may
be made of the last specification, and the rights
flowing from the duty it denotes, it could never
equal that which would be made of the second,
nor, in either case, could this evil equal that which
would arise from the adoption of the first alternative,—which indeed describes a state of things
that could scarcely exist. Civil government then,
in its worst shape, is the least of three evils, one
or other of which is unavoidable.

It has been strangely proposed as an explanation of the right of control now under consideration, that a *compact* is presumed betwixt the ruler
and subject; as if a compact could possibly be
presumed against the open refusal of one of the
parties to enter into such compact, implied in
every case of resistance to civil authority. It may
indeed be pleaded that though the party openly
resists a particular exercise of compulsion, as
what is against his present will, yet the compact
may be presumed to have been previously entered
into, leaving him now no power to retract. But
the notion of *presuming* a compact at all, without
some *act* expressive of the parties' consent,* seems

* Nor is it sufficient to tell us that a man, by voluntarily
staying in the country when he might remove out of it, tacitly
agrees to submit to its laws. To leave the country often may
be, and generally is, an intolerable hardship of itself. This

of itself a palpable absurdity: unless it merely means the presuming, from the known motives and principles that actuate, or should actuate an intelligent and moral agent, that he would have done so had he acted after a rational manner. In other words, we may assume that it would have been right, and proper, and reasonable, in a man, to make such a compact; and therefore that we have now a right to hold him to it, whether he will or not. This I take to be only a more round-about way of stating, as I have done, that a right may exist, directly and originally, to *compel* a man to do his *duty*.

If my neighbour's house should take fire in his absence, I should probably employ people to bring water to quench it, presuming that this is precisely what my friend would have wished me to do, and that he would thankfully repay me the expense incurred. But should he refuse to repay me, and were I to sue him at law, would any judge listen to the plea of a presumed *compact*,* and ground my right to repayment upon this compact? If he gave effect to my claim at all, would it not be on the general ground, that it

solution then says that it is throwing *no* hardship on a man to give him a *choice* of hardships.

* Perhaps this might be done; as there are in legal practice fictions more violent. It is allowed however that fictions are always unnecessary. It is impossible that a legal decision can be a just one, and yet want true grounds.

would be a *right thing* for every person, in similar circumstances, to act as I had done ; that beneficial effects would result from this ; that it would *be* right that expenses so incurred — subject no doubt to certain conditions and limitations—should be repaid ; and consequently that the party who should make the outlay, would *have* a direct right to be repaid ?

The difficulty supposed to attach, in theory, to the right of rulers to make use of compulsion with their subjects, seems to me to have arisen from a neglect of the distinction between the absolute truth of a moral proposition, and the suitableness of this proposition as a specification of practical duty.

The axiom above laid down, that " whatever it is obligatory on a moral agent to do, it is fit he should be compelled to do," must of course be understood only to this purpose, that this compulsion upon the agent, as an effect, and *in itself*, is a *fit* effect — one that is agreeable to our moral faculties — one in regard to which we feel that the party thus compelled suffers nothing but what he *ought* to have suffered — whether the particular party who made use of the compulsion might have had a right to do so or not. But though strictly true, as a moral proposition, that a moral agent ought to be compelled to do his duty, it is not admissible as the *specification* of a branch of human conduct, that other agents in general ought to use such compulsion : and this merely because the specification would be misapplied : in other words, men acting so as to produce this fit effect, (that of every one's being compelled to do his duty,) that is to say, acting as they would suppose, or persuade themselves, or pretend,* that this effect would be produced, would in reality not produce it, but produce an incalculable degree of mischief in its stead.

Now so strongly does the inadmissibility of this *specification*, as of a practical moral duty or right, appear to our minds, that, in our repugnance to it, we reject the truth of the abstract proposition ; and see something so dreadful in men's having the right of forcibly controlling one another's actions, associated as this right is in our minds with the idea of the flagrant abuse that would be made of it, that we find a difficulty in allowing its existence even in the abstract, or in circumstances where the danger of abuse admits of being more or less provided against ; — where, at all events, the mischief to be apprehended from the abuse of the rule, is infinitely smaller than what would arise from the want of it, or the substitution of any other.

It appears to me then that the inquiry in re-

---

* We must hold in view, as formerly stated, that a moral rule must be supposed as answering some purpose : in the present case, for instance, we must suppose that men would not always openly break a rule, where they would yet pervert one.

gard to the theory of civil government, has generally been commenced at the wrong end. It has
been assumed as being the *primary* apprehension
of our minds on this subject, that no one agent
can have a right to *control* the actions of another,
but in defence against a personal injury; and
hence the right assumed by civil governors has
been made to appear a matter requiring explanation. On the contrary, what appears to me the
primary judgment, is, that *any* agent has the right
of compelling another to do what is obligatory on
that other to do; and that this judgment is only
corrected by the consideration of the enormous
abuse that would be made of such a right if fully
recognized: while, on the other hand, a prospect
of the dreadful consequences that would ensue, if
the right existed nowhere, drives us on the institution of civil government: and according as men
rate the one danger or the other, they are disposed
to restrict or extend the powers of government.
But no one would be for restricting a government
from compelling subjects, in every particular, to
do their duty — could he only be assured that
government would *hold there.*

Children, and ignorant people, are always pleased
to see the strong hand employed, and employed
even by unauthorized individuals, in the punishment of villany, in enforcing redress of injuries,
and even in compelling the performance of positive duties of benevolence or charity. It is only

the more reflecting who, by speculating on the consequences of a general permission to this effect, are more willing that failures in moral duty should be allowed, than that performance should be enforced by irregular means. But the dissatisfaction of the most intelligent, the most reflecting, and scrupulous judge, has reference, in such cases, not to the *effect* — meaning thereby the *compulsion* or the *punishment* endured — but to the *means* by which the effect is produced. The *effect*, in the individual case, is morally *right* and *fit:* the *means*, as representing a *species* of action that would produce a bad effect, — improper and wrong.

When a miser is beheld to hoard up, or a spendthrift to dissipate, the wealth that would afford relief to his starving neighbours, what is the first judgment of an untutored mind in the case? that they *ought* to be *compelled* to part with some of their superfluities. Is it not a posterior reflection that suggests the impossibility of finding any one to whom the power of employing such compulsion could safely be trusted, and the consequent necessity of prohibiting all external interference?

A man, then, over whom a forcible control is exercised, even as regards his private actions, or the disposal of his undoubted property, does not necessarily suffer a violation of his right, in respect of what is thus *done to him*, though he may, in

respect of *him who does it :* this latter having no
right to interfere so : — always supposing however (for this is indispensable to the truth of the
case) that compulsion is exercised only for the
enforcement of *some clear moral obligation previously binding the party so compelled.* — Nor can
I in this respect admit, except in degree, the distinction between what is called perfect and imperfect obligations, and their correspondent rights.
Civil government does not allow the enforcing of
a perfect right by a private individual ; yet no one
doubts that the law of nature gives this allowance.
On the other hand, civil government does admit
the public enforcement of an imperfect right — as
in enacting a compulsory provision for the poor ;
and also in interfering in the treatment pursued
by its subjects towards third parties, as in the
abolition of the slave trade ; laws against cruelty
to animals,* and the like.   From which the inference is this, — that the limitation of the *right,*
in any case, to compel an agent to do what is obligatory on him, arises not from any natural deficiency in the right, but from an apprehension that
its exercise would be abused to the production of
more mischief than could arise from the prohibition of its exercise. — No one ever supposed a
compact between the Deity and his creatures, or
between parents and children ; yet it is impossible

* It is difficult to see how the notion of a compact could be
applied to these cases.

to deduce, as is generally done, the right in question from creation in the one case, or from pro-creation, in the other. No one would say that the Creator has a *right* to inflict gratuitous undeserved misery on his creatures, or a parent on his children, (unless it were said to *be right* to do so,) merely from their relation as Creator and parents respectively; while, on the other hand, their right to inflict just punishment, or salutary pain, or to enforce the performance of obligation, would exist independently of such relation.*

On the whole then, I should say, that the institution of civil government is not the creation of a new species of right, not even the *extension* of any right, but the *limitation* (for reasons of expediency) of a right otherwise universally existing — the right, namely, which, abstractly speaking, every moral agent has to *compel* another to do what on the latter is *morally obligatory*, what he *ought* to do, what it *is right* he should do.

The notion that civil government is a species of voluntary compact between the governors and the governed, and that a man cannot, *by right*, be subjected to government unless by his own voluntary consent, has introduced a considerable error into many modern speculations on this subject — I mean that of maintaining, as a first principle of

* Any one who had the charge of a child, would assume the right of *compelling* it to take necessary medicines, or to submit to a surgical operation, if its preservation required it.

government, that every man come to years of understanding has a right to vote for his representative in the national council. I certainly shall not say that this is not a *true* proposition — (whether it is or is not, is a question in politics, as a practical art, with which I am at present taking no concern)—but this I shall say, that it is not a *first principle* in the science of government. If it is true at all, it is true only as a deduction from this principle, that political power should be distributed in that manner in which its exercise will be most beneficial to the state. If it can be shewn, as matter of fact, either from experience or by general reasoning (which, for ought that I know, it may) that the most beneficial government would be that where universal suffrage was allowed, then I should have no hesitation in maintaining that every man — and, if any one pleases, every woman and child — should have a vote; — but not unless this is shewn. It can only be true that every man *has* a right to a suffrage, if it is true that it *is* right that he should have a suffrage. It can only be true that it *is right* that every one should have a suffrage, if it is true that this would be *beneficial to the community.* For the same reason I should be ready to maintain that if it were true (which of course it never could be) that a despotism was the most beneficial form of government, then no man but the despot would have a right to any political influence. For, upon the supposition that the government of the despot would be the most beneficial, it would surely be right that he alone should possess all political power — which I consider the same as saying that he and no other would have a right to political power.

If every man has a right to vote for his representative, every man has a right to say that he does not choose to have a representative — that he chooses to have no government at all — that he chooses to govern himself. How do you assume that there ought to be a representative government at all? You take this for granted, and then say, every man has a right to share in the appointment of representatives. A representative government, you will perhaps tell us, is the best system of government. Granted. But why? Because it is the most beneficial. But if we are to take a representative government because it is the most beneficial, shall we not, for the same reason, make a limitation of the right of suffrage, if that is most beneficial? Perhaps you will say it is not because a representative government is the most beneficial that it is the best, but because it is the only practicable method of distributing to every man that share of political power which is his natural right. But, I must repeat, there is no way in which you can prove that there ought to be political power or civil government *at all*, in which it may not be possible to prove that there ought to be a limitation of suffrage — no way in which you can prove a universal right of suffrage, in which it may not be possible to prove a universal right of declining subjection to government altogether.

"The divine right of kings"—"the divine right of constables"— "the natural inalienable right of every man to have a voice in the making of those laws by which he is to be governed" — all these rights seem to me to stand upon precisely the same level in this respect, that each exists, or does not exist, solely as its existence would be beneficial, or not beneficial.　Undoubtedly *beneficial* here means—beneficial to the whole and to every part; and since subjection to the power of others (implied in a man's having himself no political power in a community) is in itself an evil, that evil should not, unless for imperious reasons, be imposed on any member of a community, or the opposite good (a share of political influence) withheld.　But to suppose the right of civil government *at all*, is to suppose that the evil in question must be imposed, the opposite good withheld, in some degree; and the same considerations which make this necessary in a certain degree, may—(I do not say they do)—make it necessary to the utmost extent.

But though the *right* of rulers to control the actions of their subjects for the good of the community, does not rest on any sort of compact, their *power* to do so must generally be founded on some *concurrence*, either positive or negative, on the part of other members of such community.

It is obvious that if one man can overpower each one of a thousand, he can overpower the whole thousand,—provided that no two or more of them combine their strength against him. Such combination may fail to take place, either from the indifference of each man as to the measures pursued by the powerful party towards the others, or from approbation of these measures. This I would call a *negative* compact.

On the other hand, the way in which any one party thus becomes able to overpower every other individual, singly taken, of the community, is by *combination* with other parties for this purpose, whose united strength thus overbalances the un-supported power of every other individual. This may be called the positive *compact;* but it is sel-dom entered into so much with views of general benefit to the community, as of private aggrandize-ment to the immediate actors; and can in no way be identified with any compact imagined to be entered into between the bulk of the community and those who rule over them, conveying to the latter the peculiar *rights* of rulers.

The notion of a *compact*, then, may explain the power, but not the right of rulers to control their subjects ; nor can a civil government possibly be formed without some sort of agreement more or less, either positive or negative, among the members of the community.

From this follow two very important practical considerations in relation to the duty of citizens, first, where a government is yet to be established, and secondly, where an established government seems to be such a one as ought to be subverted.

I. One of the chief ends of government itself is, as we have seen, to secure, by means of a single agency directing the conduct of numbers, the execution of those designs which depend upon a combination of acts. But the formation of a government is what, by the very nature of the case, must be effected previously to the existence of a governing head—in other words, by the spontaneous combination of the actors. The practical lesson resulting from this, is the necessity of moderation in urging individual views. Where there are a multitude of parties, there must be a variety both of opinions and interests; many of which must be sacrificed before a settled order of things can be established at all; and it is not in any way possible to hope that the order which will eventually take place, will either be absolutely the best that could have been, or entirely conformable to the ideas of any particular portion of the community. In such a case, then, it is the most indispensable duty of every man to exhibit as great a degree of compliance and flexibility, and to consent to as great sacrifices of individual judgment and interest, as can be distinguished from a concurrence in measures obviously criminal and insufferable; and the evils of which would be reckoned superior even to those of anarchy itself.

II. The necessity of extreme caution in attempting the subversion of an established government, however corrupt, is founded on a consideration, first, of the strife, misery, and bloodshed, which may be produced, without even accomplishing the subversion of such government; secondly, the anarchy and confusion, without limit, either of time or degree, that may take place after this has been accomplished; and thirdly, the possibility that, after all, a worse, or no better government, may come in the room of that which has been displaced. The formation of a new government, as already said, must be a matter of *combination;* and among the multitude concerned in such a case, spontaneous combination is what the chances are infinitely against. Nothing therefore is more anxiously to be studied, than that even improvements of the most necessary and important kind should be brought about by constitutional means — that is, by means not inferring the removal of some *acknowledged authority*, under which that degree of concert may be promoted and enforced, which is requisite for the accomplishment of any public measure whatever. Indeed, the first step generally found necessary for the formation of a

new government, is the appointment of a pro-
visional government.

The general principle being established that
certain individuals have a *right* to govern the remaining part of a community, it next comes to be
inquired what more *specific* propositions this general one may be reduced to, namely, as regarding
the mode in which such power is to exist or be
constituted. Even in this advanced age of the
world, all that can well be said to be agreed upon
is the general principle of government. The specific principles are, at this moment, matter of fierce
contention in almost every nation of the earth.
But as the right of a governing power, in general,
is deduced from the fitness of the effects that result from the exercise of such a power, so the
right of any particular species of governing power,
as compared with the right of another, will depend on the fitness of the resulting effects in each
case respectively. But the validity of the right,
in each of these cases, is only to be considered as
comparative. The right of any particular kind of
government does not fail, because the right of
another, not having an actual existence in opposition to it, may be stronger. If it be allowed that
any kind of government is better than none, any
government has a right, more or less, to act as
such ; nor has a citizen a right to refuse obedience,
merely on the general ground that it is exacted by
a king, instead of a popular assembly, or because

the government has been fixed by chance or violence, or has not emanated directly and deliberately from the body of the people. The right to govern, in short, does not originate either in respect of any *form* of government, or of the mode in which such form has been established, any more than the right of a father to correct his children depends on the validity of his marriage with their mother, or the right of a schoolmaster to control his pupils on the regularity of his election to the office. In each of these cases, the right depends on the general propriety of such a right's being exercised, for the attainment of some beneficial end; not on the propriety of the method by which the means of exercising the right has been obtained. A man may have no right to procreate children but by a legal marriage (i. e. it may not *be right* that he should do so) but he must not therefore lose the right of governing such children, if he has in fact become a parent.

It is never to be lost sight of, however, that the duties peculiar to a state of civil government, being what may be called *duties of combination* — duties founded upon the fitness of certain effects that can only be produced by the combined agency of different individuals,*—can be only so far binding on each of the individuals concerned, as the action of that individual will, in reality, tend to pro-

---

* Individuals may here be taken as representing their class.

duce such effects : that is, as his action will be supported by the actions, necessary for this purpose, on the part of others. As elsewhere laid down, no action can be farther obligatory, than as the *effect*, in reference to which it is obligatory, *depends* upon such action — i. e. would take place with it, and would not take place without it. If it be obligatory on ten men to produce some *effect*, which one is unable to do, (for instance to save a vessel from being wrecked,) the obligation can only apply to one, on the supposition that the others are also to perform their part. In the same way, since the effects which civil government aim at producing, are not produced by the obedience of subjects, but by the obedience of subjects *jointly* with the endeavours of rulers to promote the benefit of the community — if rulers do not act with such a view, or act in a manner contrary to it, the obligation of subjects ceases ; — as much as the obligation of mariners to obey the commander of a vessel would cease, were it evident that his orders did not relate to the safe management of the vessel at all, or were calculated to drive her on the rocks ; or as the duty of the steersman, or any other individual mariner would cease, were his act unsupported by those acts on the part of others, which could alone give it *effect.*

It is the circumstance now adverted to, that has principally given countenance to the notion of a social *compact.* — If the duties of the subject and ruler respectively are but *conditionally* binding, such duties are held as arising only from a compact of the parties. But this does not follow. Obligation sometimes arises from the intrinsic fitness of an effect; sometimes from the passing of a promise : *conditions* are not peculiar to either case ; but may exist, or be wanting, in any one of the two, as well as in the other. I may be bound by a promise, made without a condition, to perform an act not essentially obligatory. On the other hand, I may not be bound to perform an act essentially obligatory, but on the *condition* that my act will receive that co-operation from others, on which the production of the *effect* may depend. The duty of a subject is only of *conditional* obligation ; but the condition being performed by the other party, the obligation is *intrinsic* and independent; and though it may be increased by a previous voluntary agreement, can never fail for want of it.

In short, in the case of a *contract*, the performance of the condition by one party would not infer any obligation on the other, but for the existence of the contract: in the case of a *duty of combination*, the obligation exists originally on all the parties among whom the combination may take place ; but ceases, in regard to each one, where the others have failed in it.

To recapitulate. — The theory of civil government just means a collection of certain propositions specifying a particular class of *duties* obligatory on men to perform; which duties again involve and imply certain *rights*. To explain the theory of government, is to deduce the truth of these propositions from admitted first principles — unless, of course, so far as any of these propositions themselves may be of the nature of primary truths.

It has been shewn that whatever specification of duty is furnished to an agent, he himself must explain and apply such specification.* To prevent the abuse of such application, through ignorance, self-deceit, or wilful perversity, it is found expedient, in many circumstances, to make the specification of duty — *obedience to the directions of others.* But though this method may be pursued and varied through a series of steps, it is obvious we must at last arrive at a point which forms the verge of the scale. Do how we will, we must leave, in the hands of some persons or other, certain specifications of duties and of rights that will be subject to much and dangerous abuse; and the object of the constitution of civil government, in general, and in its details, is, simply, to confine the possibility of such abuse within the narrowest possible limits.†

* Indeed he must judge of the truth of the proposition containing the specification: but this we must, at present, suppose as agreed upon.

† One of the most effectual means that seems to come within

It is to be observed, however, that for the just and true application of every specification of duty or right, every agent is responsible in *conscience*, though he may not be responsible to other agents.

To explain this, we must divide rights into three species ; absolute rights ; rights in conscience ; and relative rights.

An *absolute* right is what is exercised in the real and true application of a moral rule or specification of duty ; and this real and true application, is what the agent is bound to discover.

A right *in conscience* is what is exercised in that application of a moral rule which an agent, to the

the reach of human ingenuity for attaining this purpose, is that beautiful contrivance in the frame-work of government, — the separation of the legislative and executive functions. The legislator makes laws for the *abstract case* — under circumstances in which it is impossible for partiality to operate. The moment he enacts the law, he loses all farther control over it. He fashions the instrument, but it is wielded by other hands than his own. His friends, as well as his enemies, his neighbours, his relatives, himself, are thenceforth subject to it — subject to it as it shall be administered by others. — The executive magistrate, again, has to deal with the particular case — is confined to the application of a law made to his hand. His prejudices and his partialities are alike restrained. The law is formed, and he has only to determine its application. — The institution of trial by jury is an extension of the same principle. The judge wields the sword of the law ; but he wields it only against those whom the verdict of the jury places within his reach.

best of his means of discovering, believes its real and true application.

A *relative* right is that, the exercise of which, in whatever way an agent may apply the specification of it, no *other* agent has a right to prevent.

In practice, an absolute right, and a right in conscience, must stand for the same. I shall therefore include the latter in the former denomination.

A man has a right, relatively to his neighbours — who have no right to prevent him — to spend his money as he pleases. He has an absolute right only to do so in a prudent and useful manner.

A man has a right to correct his children as he pleases, relatively to other men; but a right in conscience, and as a responsible being, only so far as may be necessary for purposes of moral discipline and improvement.*

* On a neglect of the distinction between an absolute, and a relative right, was founded an argument employed some years ago in the House of Lords, against Catholic emancipation; and in the efficacy of which the opposers of that measure seemed to find considerable ground of triumph. It was simply this, that every government has a *right* to take such measures as it *judges necessary* for its own preservation : consequently, if government *should determine* that Catholic emancipation was *dangerous to its existence*, it had a valid *right* to refuse emancipation. — Now this was just the same as if a judge on the bench should defend an iniquitous decision by saying, " I have a *right* to determine this matter in the way which *I may deem just ;* and as I have pronounced that this is just, I have

It is obvious that two *absolute* rights, on the part of different individuals, can never oppose one another. Rights in conscience may, — so long as the opinions and consciences of men differ. Two persons may each conscientiously judge himself to have right to the sovereignty of a nation: subjects may at once conscientiously oppose their rulers, and rulers enforce their commands on subjects. For this there is no remedy, but that of enlightening the judgments and consciences of men, and reducing to the greatest possible degree of precision, the specification of their duty — which is the province of the practical moralist. The obligation of subjects to obey, seems at first view contradictory to their right to oppose their rulers. The contradiction would be solved by more *specific* forms of stating the obligation and right.

only done what I had a right to do, and no one has a right to complain;"— in other words, because the parties have not a *right* to prevent the judge from passing such a sentence, therefore it is a just sentence. Is it not plain that whatever might be the right of the judge, as relative to the parties, his right absolutely, and in conscience, was only to make such a decision as to the best of his belief was just? and is it not equally plain, that though the argument against Catholic emancipation might be conclusive against those who should maintain generally that the state had no right to exclude any of its subjects from its privileges, honours and employment, whatever apprehension of danger might exist, it could not operate against those who *denied the danger altogether.* The reality of the *danger*, not that of the *right*, was the point at issue.

At present it may be sufficient to observe, that there is, in practice, little difficulty in distinguishing between those cases in which a subject ought to submit to a command, against his individual judgment as to the propriety of that command, and those cases where he may safely trust his own judgment in deciding upon resistance ; just in the same way as the general propriety of a man's adhering closely to the directions of a physician, whether he perceives their fitness or not, is not inconsistent with his exercising a judgment as to the talents and conduct of any particular physician, and even dismissing him if he sees cause. In general, the actual external checks that repress the right of resistance in subjects is a sufficient guarantee against any abuse of the theoretical principle.

The wickedness of men will always occasion instances of opposition between relative rights. So long as the right of rulers to use compulsion with their subjects exists at all, it will be used for purposes of oppression; so long as the right of subjects exists, in any circumstance, to resist authority, it will be rendered the pretext for insubordination. This can never be greatly bettered by improving moral *rules*, but by making *men* better.

CHAPTER V.

THEORY OF PROPERTY.

THE nature of *property* is to be explained from the general *axiom*,—that it is *wrong to occasion pain or uneasiness:* * it being laid down, at the same time, as another axiom, — that, in the nature of things, it must occasion *pain or uneasiness* to deprive a person either of what is a *source* of present ease, comfort, or enjoyment ; or what he intends, or expects to draw enjoyment from in future. †   To take away any enjoyment, or to occasion actual pain, only differ in this, that the two things are in different parts of the scale — both making the state of a being worse : and the loss of an enjoyment must occasion some degree of positive pain in the mind of the being who suffers the loss.   It is obligatory then not to inflict that pain — a person has a right that that pain should not be inflicted ; i. e. that he should not lose his property.

* Ax. II.   † Ax. XXIII.

The word *property* is ambiguous. It sometimes merely means, what a man actually *possesses*, sometimes what he has a *right* to possess, or what it is wrong to take from him. In the second sense, it is plain that to ask why a man has a right to his property, why it is wrong to deprive him of it, is just to ask, why a man has a right to that which he has a right to — why it is wrong to take from a man what it is wrong to take from him — which is absurd.

The only rational question then is, why has a man a *right* to that of which he is in *possession?* why is it *wrong* to deprive him of it? and this is the question I have answered, by saying, that it is because the depriving him of it must occasion him pain or uneasiness.

For I can attach no other meaning to the *possession* of any thing (that could be held to constitute property,) than either that a man is presently enjoying a benefit from something, or intends or expects to draw some benefit from it; hence, whatever sensibly indicates this intention, is held to constitute the act of taking, occupying, holding, possessing, keeping, — such as grasping in the hand, or seizing in the arms; bearing on the body, or attaching to it; proclaiming by words, marks, or writing; fixing a residence near, and the like. Hence these *acts* are said to create a right of property, that is, to make it wrong that the thing should be taken away: because they indicate an *intention* and *expectation* of enjoying the property, which expectation the taking away of it must necessarily disappoint, and thence occasion pain.

But it occasions *pain* to deprive a man of property unjustly held : is it therefore wrong to take it from him and restore it to the right owner ?

To occasion pain is, *in the abstract*, wrong : (see first remark subjoined to *axioms*.) But here, to spare the pain, even if *undeserved*, to one, is to leave it lying on another who had a *prior* right to escape it. And a right which would involve the violation of a prior right, is no right.

The next question then is — can any right exist *anterior* to, or *co-equal* with, first possession ?

Now there is no obvious or unquestionable *fitness* that any one being, rather than another, should possess a particular portion of what does not, in its nature, admit of being shared by all alike, such as land, fruit-trees, wild animals, &c. &c. It follows that first possession does not wrong another, but the violation of actual possession wrongs him who does possess. The violation of property then in these cases occasions wrong, without the necessary justification of removing a greater wrong.

If land admitted of being shared by all men alike, there would be an original fitness in each man's having his share : * from which of course might be deduced the original *right* of each to

* Ax. IV.

have his share. The first occupation then, by any one, of more than his share, would be a violation of another right, and restitution would be justly due.

And though there be no obvious and unquestionable fitness that any one man should possess this or that portion of land more than another, and consequently no right in any one to deprive a man of what he has actually become possessed of, in the *bonâ fide* belief that he thereby injured no previous right; yet there may be a fitness why lands as yet unoccupied, or left vacant by decease of a former occupant, should be distributed or destined in one particular way rather than another. It is undoubtedly fit that property should be distributed so that much benefit may be derived from it rather than little; so that the benefit may be equally rather than unequally shared.*

In the discussions that have arisen in regard to the question, how far the right of property is founded on views of general utility, two very different things have always been entirely confounded; namely, the *negative* and the *positive* right of property, which may exist either together or in opposition.

In the case of first possession of land, &c., as above explained, the right is of the negative kind; because what a man is possessed of merely by first occupation, is *his*, or he has a right to it, in no

* Ax. I. VII. IV.

other way than as it is *wrong* to take it from him; because doing so does him hurt. Now this right is founded in utility, only in the sense in which a man's right not to be maimed or wounded is founded in utility. But the fitness why land should be enjoyed by some, rather than by none; why it should be distributed or succeeded to in this, or that way, is founded on views of general utility, previously to actual possession by any one; and here a positive right of property is constituted, in consequence of which it is wrong to deprive the possessor, not merely, as in the former instance, because it is wrong to occasion him pain, but because there is a *positive fitness* why he, rather than another, should enjoy the benefit. In the one case, this piece of land is a man's property because it is wrong to deprive him of it; in the other case, it is wrong to deprive him of it, because it is his property. And it is obvious that both reasons may, in any particular case, exist together.

The superior right which a man has to the fruits of his own labour, is deducible from the same principles as the other rights of property.

In the first place, what a man creates himself, he must be the first possessor of.

But in the next place, besides the pain and uneasiness of being deprived of any thing held in possession — that is, any thing which a man indicates that he is receiving, or expecting benefit from, and therefore wishes to keep,—there is, in depriv-

ing a man of that which he has impended pains
and labour in procuring, *the gratuitous infliction of*
that pain and labour upon him : for the positive infliction of an evil is evidently nothing different
from the taking away of that which an evil has been
endured to obtain.

Mr. Dugald Stewart (Phil. of Act. and Mor.
Powers,*) maintains, that, previously to the establishment of civil laws, the impending of labour is
the *only* foundation of property.   He allows, however, apparently in contradiction to this, the right
which actual present *possession* imparts; and for
the rest, the instances he adduces in support of his
doctrine only prove that, in a state of nature, the
right of property is held to cease where a thing is
abandoned *without any indication of an intention*
to keep it ; for they do not prove that the
mere leaving or removing from a possession is
held to be a surrender of the right of property,
where any indication is made of an intention to
resume it.   This intention or purpose is just that
which makes the right to be perceived, and that
without which, of course, it cannot appear to exist.

* Book IV. Supplement to Chap. II.

END OF VOL. I.